ROESCH LIBRARY
UNIVERSITY OF DAYTON

THE LETTER TO PHILEMON

VOLUME 34C

THE ANCHOR BIBLE is a fresh approach to the world's greatest classic. Its object is to make the Bible accessible to the modern reader; its method is to arrive at the meaning of biblical literature through exact translation and extended exposition, and to reconstruct the ancient setting of the biblical story, as well as the circumstances of its transcription and the characteristics of its transcribers.

THE ANCHOR BIBLE is a project of international and interfaith scope: Protestant, Catholic, and Jewish scholars from many countries contribute individual volumes. The project is not sponsored by any ecclesiastical organization and is not intended to reflect any particular theological doctrine. Prepared under our joint supervision, THE ANCHOR BIBLE is an effort to make available all the significant historical and linguistic knowledge which bears on the interpretation of the biblical record.

THE ANCHOR BIBLE is aimed at the general reader with no special formal training in biblical studies; yet it is written with the most exacting standards of scholarship, reflecting the highest technical accomplishment.

This project marks the beginning of a new era of cooperation among scholars in biblical research, thus forming a common body of knowledge to be shared by all.

William Foxwell Albright
David Noel Freedman
GENERAL EDITORS

THE ANCHOR BIBLE

THE LETTER TO PHILEMON

◆

A New Translation
with Introduction and Commentary

JOSEPH A. FITZMYER, S.J.

THE ANCHOR BIBLE
Doubleday
New York London Toronto Sydney Auckland

THE ANCHOR BIBLE
PUBLISHED BY DOUBLEDAY
a division of Random House, Inc.
1540 Broadway, New York, New York 10036

IMPRIMI POTEST
Very Reverend James R. Stormes, S.J.
Praepositus Provinciae Marylandiae

IMPRIMATUR
Most Reverend William E. Lori, S.T.D.
Vicar General for the Archdiocese of Washington
Washington, D.C.
6 January 2000

The *imprimatur* is an official declaration that a book is free of doctrinal or moral error. No implication is contained therein that the one who has granted the *imprimatur* agrees with the content, opinions, or statements expressed.

Library of Congress Cataloging-in-Publication Data

Bible. N.T. Philemon. English. Fitzmyer. 2000.
The letter to Philemon: a new translation with introduction and commentary / Joseph A. Fitzmyer.—1st ed.
p. cm.—(The Anchor Bible; v. 34C)
Includes bibliograpical references and indexes.
1. Bible. N.T. Philemon—Commentaries. I. Fitzmyer, Joseph A. II. Title. III. Bible. English. Anchor Bible. 1964; v. 34C.

BS192.2.A1 1964.G3 vol. 34c
[BS2765.3]
220.7′7s—dc21
[227′.86077] 00-029501

ISBN 0-385-49629-X

Printed in the United States of America
December 2000
First Edition
10 9 8 7 6 5 4 3 2 1

To
students whom I have taught over the years
since 1958
from whom I have learned much

CONTENTS

◆

CONTENTS

INDEXES

PREFACE

◆

After I had finished the commentary on the Acts of the Apostles for the Anchor Bible series, the editor, D. N. Freedman, asked me to write a commentary on Paul's Letter to Philemon. It was supposed to be written by another contributor who died before he could complete it. Having written two very brief commentaries on this Pauline letter in the *Jerome Biblical Commentary* (1968) and in the *New Jerome Biblical Commentary* (1990), I was happy to comply with the editor's request.

Once again, this commentary on the Letter to Philemon is like the others that I have written in this series, on the Gospel according to Luke, the Acts of the Apostles, and Paul's Epistle to the Romans. It purports to be written in the classic style of biblical commentaries using the historical-critical method, which is considered the best way to ascertain the sense intended and expressed by a biblical writer, or to arrive at what is usually called the literal sense of a biblical writing.

The Letter to Philemon is a very brief Pauline writing, containing only twenty-five verses, 335 Greek words, and 143 different vocables, but it has some problematic aspects that have always been the object of no little discussion. Chief among them is why such a letter, addressed to an individual whom Paul knew, ever found its way into the Christian biblical canon. By including it, early Christians have passed it on as part of their heritage to coming generations of Christian readers.

Earlier commentaries on the Letter to Philemon will be mentioned by the name of their authors and an abbreviated form of their titles, which are listed fully in the general bibliography. In that bibliography the commentators are broken down into groups according to time: patristic commentators (Greek and Latin writers, listed chronologically); medieval commentators (Greek and Latin writers, listed chronologically); fifteenth- to eighteenth-century commentators (listed chronologically); and nineteenth- and twentieth-century commentators (listed alphabetically). It has been my aim to give as complete a list of commentaries on the Letter to Philemon as I have been able to find. Many medieval commentaries have never been published; they are found in manuscript form in European libraries. If I have come across reference to them, I include the information to the extent that it seemed accurate. In the specific bibliographies at the end of the introduction or at the end of pericopes, authors are listed in alphabetical order. When a strange or unfamiliar name appears in the COMMENTS or NOTES, the reader should consult first the specific bibliography at the end of the pericope; if the information is not found there, then the bibliography of the introduction and the general bibliography should be consulted. In the latter, not only commentaries are listed but also monographs and articles on general topics pertaining to the letter. The index of modern authors may also serve as a guide to information about the writers of books and articles.

References to OT books cite the chapter and verses according to the Hebrew or Aramaic text, which may not be that of some English Bibles. This is to be noted especially in the case of the Psalter, where psalms are always cited according to the numbering of the Hebrew text, even when the discussion may involve the Greek form of the text in the LXX. In case of doubt, one can usually consult the NAB, which uses the Hebrew-text numbering.

Lastly, it is my duty to acknowledge my debt to the editor of the Anchor Bible series, David Noel Freedman, for his initial suggestion that I write this commentary and for his subsequent help and advice in its writing. I am also grateful to Dr. Mark J. H. Fretz and Mr. Andrew Corbin, the in-house editors at Doubleday, and to the copy editor, Bill Betts, for their concern and assistance in turning my manuscript into a book.

Joseph A. Fitzmyer, S.J.
Professor Emeritus of Biblical Studies
The Catholic University of America
Washington, D.C. 20064
Resident at:
Jesuit Community, Georgetown University
P.O. Box 571200
Washington, D.C. 20057-1200

ABBREVIATIONS

◆

AB — Anchor Bible
ABD — D. N. Freedman (ed)., *The Anchor Bible Dictionary* (6 vols.; New York: Doubleday, 1992)
ABRL — Anchor Bible Reference Library
ACNT — American Commentary on the New Testament
ACW — Ancient Christian Writers
AnBib — Analecta biblica
ANRW — *Aufstieg und Niedergang der römischen Welt* (95 vols.; ed. H. Temporini and W. Haase; Berlin and New York: de Gruyter, 1972–)
AsSeign — *Assemblées du Seigneur*
ASTI — *Annual of the Swedish Theological Institute*
ATR — *Anglican Theological Review*
b. — Babylonian Talmud (prefixed to the name of a tractate)
BAC — Biblioteca de autores cristianos
BAGD — W. Bauer, W. F. Arndt, and F. W. Gingrich, *A Greek-English Lexicon of the New Testament and Other Early Christian Literature* (2d ed., rev. F. W. Gingrich and F. W. Danker; Chicago: University of Chicago, 1979)
BA^6 — W. Bauer, *Griechisch-deutsches Wörterbuch zu den Schriften des Neuen Testaments und der frühchristlichen Literatur* (6th ed., rev. K. and B. Aland; Berlin: de Gruyter, 1988)
BBB — Bonner biblische Beiträge
BDF — F. Blass and A. Debrunner, *A Greek Grammar of the New Testament and Other Early Christian Literature* (tr. R. W. Funk; Chicago: University of Chicago, 1961)
BDR — F. Blass and A. Debrunner, *Grammatik des neutestamentlichen Griechisch* (14th ed.; ed. F. Rehkopf; Göttingen: Vandenhoeck & Ruprecht, 1976)
BibLeb — *Bibel und Leben*
BJRL — *Bulletin of the John Rylands (University) Library (of Manchester)*
BR — *Biblical Research*
BSac — *Bibliotheca Sacra*

BT	*The Bible Translator*
BU	Biblische Untersuchungen
BVC	*Bible et vie chrétienne*
BWANT	Beiträge zur Wissenschaft vom Alten und Neuen Testament
BZ	*Biblische Zeitschrift*
BZNW	Beihefte zur ZNW
CahEv	*Cahiers évangile*
CB	*Cultura bíblica*
CBCNEB	Cambridge Bible Commentary on the New English Bible
CBQ	*Catholic Biblical Quarterly*
CBSC	Cambridge Bible for Schools and Colleges
CCLat	Corpus Christianorum, Latin series
CD	Damascus Document (from Cairo Genizah)
CentB	Century Bible
CGTC	Cambridge Greek Testament Commentary
CIG	*Corpus inscriptionum graecarum*
CIL	*Corpus inscriptionum latinarum*
ClassQ	*Classical Quarterly*
CNT	Commentaire du Nouveau Testament
ConcJ	*Concordia Journal*
CSEL	Corpus scriptorum ecclesiasticorum latinorum
CTM	*Concordia Theological Monthly*
DBSup	*Dictionnaire de la Bible, Supplément*
EDNT	H. Balz and G. Schneider (eds.), *Exegetical Dictionary of the New Testament* (3 vols.; Grand Rapids, Mich.: Eerdmans, 1990–93)
EGGNT	Exegetical Guide to the Greek New Testament
EKKNT	Evangelisch-Katholischer Kommentar zum Neuen Testament
EKL	*Evangelisches Kirchenlexikon* (5 vols.; ed. E. Falbusch et al.; Göttingen: Vandenhoeck & Ruprecht, 1986–97)
Ep.	*Epistle*
EstBíb	*Estudios bíblicos*
EvErz	*Evangelische Erziehung*
EvQ	*Evangelical Quarterly*
EvT	*Evangelische Theologie*
Expos	*Expositor*
ExpTim	*Expository Times*
FC	Fathers of the Church
GAGNT	M. Zerwick and M. Grosvenor, *A Grammatical Analysis of the Greek New Testament* (2 vols.; Rome: Biblical Institute, 1979)

GCS	Griechische christliche Schriftsteller
GSLNT	Geistliche Schriftlesung, Neues Testament
GTT	*Gereformeerd theologisch tijdschrift*
HCNT	Hand-Commentar, Neues Testament
HNT	Handbuch zum Neuen Testament
HTKNT	Herders theologischer Kommentar zum Neuen Testament
HTR	*Harvard Theological Review*
IB	G. A. Buttrick (ed.), *Interpreter's Bible* (12 vols.; Nashville, Tenn., and New York: Abingdon, 1952–57)
IBNTG	C. F. D. Moule, *An Idiom Book of New Testament Greek* (Cambridge: Cambridge University, 1953)
ICC	International Critical Commentary
IDB	G. A. Buttrick (ed.), *Interpreter's Dictionary of the Bible* (4 vols.; Nashville, Tenn., and New York: Abingdon, 1962)
IDBSup	K. Crim (ed.), *Interpreter's Dictionary of the Bible Supplementary Volume* (Nashville, Tenn., and New York: Abingdon, 1976)
Int	*Interpretation*
JBC	R. E. Brown et al. (eds.), *The Jerome Biblical Commentary* (2 vols. in 1; Englewood Cliffs, N.J.: Prentice-Hall, 1968)
JBL	*Journal of Biblical Literature*
JR	*Journal of Religion*
JRS	*Journal of Roman Studies*
JSNT	*Journal of the Study of the New Testament*
JSNTSup	Supplements to *JSNT*
JTS	*Journal of Theological Studies*
KEHNT	Kurzgefasstes exegetisches Handbuch zum Neuen Testament
KJV	King James Version (Authorized Version of the Bible of 1611)
KNT	Kommentar zum Neuen Testament
k.t.l.	*kai ta loipa* (= et cetera)
LCL	Loeb Classical Library
LQ	*Lutheran Quarterly*
LSJ	H. G. Liddell, R. Scott, and H. S. Jones, A *Greek-English Lexicon* (2 vols.; 9th ed.; Oxford: Clarendon, 1940)
LW	*Luther's Works*
LXX	Septuagint
MeyerK	H. A. W. Meyer, *Kritisch-exegetischer Kommentar über das Neue Testament* (Göttingen: Vandenhoeck & Ruprecht, 1847–)
MM	J. H. Moulton and G. Milligan, *The Vocabulary of the Greek Testament Illustrated from Papyri and Other Non-*

	Literary Sources (London: Hodder and Stoughton, 1930; repr. 1957)
MNTC	Moffatt New Testament Commentary
MS(S)	Manuscript(s)
MT	Masoretic text (Hebrew text of the OT)
MUSJ	*Mélanges de l'Université Saint-Joseph*
N-A[27]	B. and K. Aland (eds.), *Novum Testamentum graece* (27th ed.; Stuttgart: Deutsche Bibelgesellschaft, 1993)
NAB	New American Bible
NCentBC	New Century Bible Commentary
NClarB	New Clarendon Bible
NDIEC	G. H. R. Horsley and S. R. Llewelyn (eds.), *New Documents Illustrating Early Christianity* (8 vols.; North Ryde, N.S.W.: Ancient History Documentary Research Centre; Grand Rapids, Mich.: Eerdmans, 1976–98)
NEB	New English Bible
NICNT	New International Commentary on the New Testament
NIDNTT	C. Brown (ed.), *The New International Dictionary of New Testament Theology* (3 vols.; Grand Rapids, Mich.: Zondervan, 1975–78)
NIV	New International Version (of the Bible)
NJB	New Jerusalem Bible
NJBC	R. E. Brown et al. (eds.), *The New Jerome Biblical Commentary* (Englewood Cliffs, N.J.: Prentice-Hall, 1990)
NovT	*Novum Testamentum*
NovTSup	Supplements to *NovT*
NRSV	New Revised Standard Version (of the Bible)
NT	New Testament
NTAbh	Neutestamentliche Abhandlungen
NTD	Das Neue Testament deutsch
NTF	Neutestamentliche Forschungen
NTS	*New Testament Studies*
NTSR	The New Testament for Spiritual Reading
NTTS	New Testament Tools and Studies
OT	Old Testament
ÖTBKNT	Ökumenischer Taschenbuch-Kommentar zum Neuen Testament
P.	*Papyrus*
PAHT	J. A. Fitzmyer, *Paul and His Theology* (Englewood Cliffs, N.J.: Prentice-Hall, 1989)
PG	J. Migne, Patrologia Graeca
PL	J. Migne, Patrologia Latina
PLSup	Supplements to PL

PRS	*Perspectives in Religious Studies*
PSB	*La Sainte Bible de Pirot-Clamer* (12 vols.; Paris: Letouzey et Ané, 1938, repr. 1946; 3d ed., 1951)
PW	*Paulys Real-Encyclopädie der classischen Altertumswissenschaft* (Neue Bearbeitung, ed. G. Wissowa; Stuttgart: Metzler, 1905–78)
RB	*Revue biblique*
REB	Revised English Bible
ResQ	*Restoration Quarterly*
RevBén	*Revue Bénédictine*
RevExp	*Review and Expositor*
RevistB	*Revista bíblica*
RF	*Razón y fe*
RGG[3]	*Religion in Geschichte und Gegenwart* (3d ed.; 7 vols.; Tübingen: Mohr [Siebeck], 1957–65)
RHPR	*Revue d'histoire et de philosophie religieuses*
RHR	*Revue de l'histoire des religions*
RivB	*Rivista biblica*
RNT	Regensburger Neues Testament
RSV	Revised Standard Version (of the Bible)
SBJ	*La Sainte Bible de Jérusalem*
SBLDS	Society of Biblical Literature Dissertation Series
SBLSP	Society of Biblical Literature Seminar Papers
SBS	Stuttgarter Bibel-Studien
SBT	Studies in Biblical Theology
SC	Sources chrétiennes
ScCatt	*Scuola cattolica*
SNT	Studien zum Neuen Testament
SNTSMS	Studiorum Novi Testamenti Societas Monograph Series
SPCIC	*Studiorum paulinorum congressus internationalis catholicus 1961* (AnBib 17–18; Rome: Biblical Institute, 1963)
SPIB	Scripta Pontificii Instituti Biblici
Str-B	(H. Strack and) P. Billerbeck, *Kommentar zum Neuen Testament aus Talmud und Midrasch* (6 vols.; Munich: Beck, 1926–63)
TAPS	Transactions of the American Philosophical Society
TBT	*The Bible Today*
TCGNT	B. M. Metzger, *Textual Commentary of the Greek New Testament* (2d ed.; Stuttgart and New York: United Bible Societies, 1994)
TDNT	G. Kittel and G. Friedrich, *Theological Dictionary of the New Testament* (10 vols.; Grand Rapids, Mich.: Eerdmans, 1964–76)

TheolEv	*Theologia evangelica* (Pretoria)
THKNT	Theologischer Handkommentar zum Neuen Testament
ThStud	*Theologische Studiën*
TKNT	Theologischer Kommentar zum Neuen Testament
TLNT	C. Spicq, *Theological Lexicon of the New Testament* (3 vols.; Peabody, Mass.: Hendrickson, 1994)
TLZ	*Theologische Literaturzeitung*
TQ	*Theologische Quartalschrift*
TRE	*Theologische Realenzyklopädie* (29 vols. to date; Berlin: de Gruyter, 1977–)
TSK	*Theologische Studien und Kritiken*
TU	Texte und Untersuchungen
TynNTC	Tyndale New Testament Commentary
TzF	Texte zur Forschung
USQR	*Union Seminary Quarterly Review* (New York)
USR	*Union Seminary Review* (Richmond, Va.)
UTB	Uni-Taschenbücher
VC	*Vigiliae christianae*
Vg	Vulgata Latina (Vulgate version of the Bible)
VL	Vetus Latina (Old Latin version of the Bible)
vol.	volume
VS	Verbum salutis
WAusg	Weimar Ausgabe (of works of M. Luther)
WBC	Word Biblical Commentary
WD	*Wort und Dienst*
WMANT	Wissenschaftliche Monographien zum Alten und Neuen Testament
ZBG	M. Zerwick, *Biblical Greek Illustrated by Examples* (Rome: Biblical Institute, 1963)
ZNW	*Zeitschrift für die neutestamentliche Wissenschaft*
ZWT	*Zeitschrift für die wissenschaftliche Theologie*

THE LETTER TO PHILEMON: TRANSLATION

◆

1Paul, a prisoner for Christ Jesus, and Timothy, our brother, to Philemon,
our dear friend and fellow worker, 2to Apphia, our sister, to Archippus, our
fellow soldier, and to the church at your house, 3grace and peace to you from
God our Father and the Lord Jesus Christ.

4I give thanks to my God, as I always remember you in my prayers, 5because
I hear about the faith that you have in the Lord Jesus and your love for all
God's dedicated people, 6so that the sharing in your faith may be effective in
the realization of all the good that is ours in Christ. 7For I have experienced
much joy and consolation in your love, because the hearts of God's dedicated
people have been refreshed through you, my brother.

8So, although I am emboldened enough in Christ to order you to do what
is proper, 9I would rather appeal out of love. I, Paul, am an elderly man and
now a prisoner too for Christ Jesus. 10I appeal to you on behalf of my child,
Onesimus, whose father I have become in my imprisonment. 11He was once
useless to you, but now he has become quite useful [both] to you and to me.
12I am sending him, that is, my very own heart, back to you. 13I would have
preferred to keep him here with me, so that he might serve me on your behalf
during my imprisonment for the gospel; 14but I did not want to do anything
without your consent, so that the good you do might not be forced but come
of your own free will. 15For perhaps he has been separated for a while for this
very reason, that you may have him back for ever, 16no longer as a slave but as
more than a slave, as a beloved brother. He is such to me, but how much more
to you, both as a human being and in the Lord. 17If, then, you consider me
your partner, welcome him as you would welcome me. 18If he has wronged you
in any matter or owes you anything, charge that to me. 19I, Paul, write this
with my own hand; I will repay it—not to mention that you owe me even your
own self. 20Yes, my brother, may I profit from you in the Lord. Refresh my
heart in Christ!

21Confident of your acquiescence, I write to you, knowing that you will do
even more than I ask. 22At the same time, prepare a guest-room for me, for I
hope that through your prayers I may be restored to you. 23Epaphras, my fellow
prisoner in Christ Jesus, sends you his greetings, 24as do Mark, Aristarchus,
Demas, and Luke, my fellow workers. 25The grace of the Lord Jesus Christ be
with your spirit!

INTRODUCTION

◆

I. Title, Text, Authorship, Date and Place of Composition

◆

(1) Title

This Pauline letter has always been known in all Greek manuscripts of it as *Pros Philēmona,* "To Philemon," even though some manuscripts add further modifications, such as "written from Rome" or "and Apphia, masters of Onesimus, and to Archippus, the deacon of the church in Colossae," or "written from Rome from Paul through (Tychicus and) Onesimus, the house-servant." See the further variants in the NOTE on the subscriptions of the letter at the end of the commentary.

Manuscripts of the Latin Vulgate use as a title either *Ad Philemonem* or *Epistola beati Pauli apostoli ad Philemonem.* The ancient Syriac version uses "Epistle to Philemon." By such ancient titles the literary form of the writing is also partly designated, for it is in reality a letter of petition *(Bittschrift).*

(2) Text

The Greek text of the Letter to Philemon has been transmitted with remarkable sameness by copyists across the centuries. Of the twenty-five verses, eighteen are variant-free; the number of significant variant readings is minimal and scarcely reaches ten (mainly in vv 2, 6, 9, 10, 11, 12, 25). They will be mentioned in the NOTES in due course; meanwhile see *TCGNT*, 588–89. For a reaction to the use of mechanical aids in the statistical method of textual criticism, used by V. A. Dearing on the Greek text of the Letter to Philemon, see B. M. Metzger, *The Text,* 167–69. The ancient Latin and Syriac versions also reflect the stability of the original Greek text.

(3) AUTHORSHIP

From Marcion on, the Pauline authenticity of the Letter to Philemon has been generally admitted. Marcion included the letter in his canon of the NT. According to Tertullian (*Adv. Marcionem* 5.21; [CCLat 1. 725–26]), *Soli huic epistolae brevitas sua profuit, ut falsarias manus Marcionis evaderet* (To this letter alone did its brevity avail to escape the falsifying hands of Marcion). Compare Jerome, *In Ep. ad Philemonem*, Prologue (PL 26. 638). Origen (*Hom. in Jeremiam* 19) acknowledged its Pauline authorship, and it so appears in the list of the *Muratorian Canon* §4.

Because the Letter to Philemon seemed to lack any doctrinal content, it was at times neglected in the ancient church; and some even judged that it was not written by Paul, especially in parts of the church in Syria up to the fifth century. Jerome (*In Ep. ad Philemonem*, Prologue [PL 26. 637–38]), John Chrysostom (*Argumentum in Ep. ad Philemonem* [PG 62. 702]), and Theodore of Mopsuestia (*In Ep. ad Philemonem* [ed. H. B. Swete], 2. 259–60) rose to the defense of its Pauline authorship. The ancient testimony about the letter is otherwise almost unanimous in taking it for granted that the Apostle Paul had written it.

(4) Today the authenticity of the Letter to Philemon is almost universally admitted, for there is no serious reason to question it. Moreover it is difficult to imagine why a pseudepigrapher of later date would want to concoct such a letter and pass it off as written by Paul of Tarsus. The language, vocabulary, style, and structure of the letter, as well as its argumentation, are notably Pauline (see Schenk, *ANRW*, 3443–45). "The letter, which of all Paul's letters, stands closest in form to ancient private letters, displays in its personal features the signs of a genuine true-to-life quality" (W. G. Kümmel, *Introduction*, 349–50).

(5) A few interpreters in the nineteenth century, however, did deny its authenticity: F. C. Baur, of the so-called Tübingen School, regarded it as a second-century Christian romance composed to explain how post-Pauline Christianity should deal with slavery (*Paulus*, 2. 92–93; or *Paul*, 2. 80–84). Similarly, C. Weizsäcker (*Das apostolische Zeitalter*, 545), R. Steck ("Plinius," 570–75), and the Dutch critic W. C. van Manen ("Philemon, Epistle to") called in question its Pauline authorship. H. J. Holtzmann thought that parts of the letter were interpolated ("Der Brief").

(6) In v 19 Paul speaks of writing "with my own hand." That may mean that he himself wrote the whole letter. It could also mean that at a certain point in his dictation to a scribe or amanuensis he snatched the pen and wrote a few words of that verse (see NOTE on v 19). That detail, however, cannot be utilized in the discussion about the authenticity of the Letter to Philemon

as a whole, because that could be a literary device to make it sound authentic. The judgment about the Paline authenticity of the letter does not depend on that verse.

(7) The Letter to Philemon is related to the Epistle to the Colossians, which likewise bears Paul's name and has Timothy as the cosender (Col 1:1), in which Paul appears as a prisoner (Col 4:3, 10, 18), and in which both Archippus and Onesimus are mentioned (Col 4:9, 17). Moreover five of those who send greetings in the Letter to Philemon (vv 23–24) are also listed among the six who do so in the Epistle to the Colossians (4:10–14). The Onesimus who accompanies Tychicus on his mission to Colossae (Col 4:7–9) is the person who is the object of Paul's Letter to Philemon. Hence details in these letters relate them to each other in a way that is almost unique in the Pauline corpus.

Knox maintained that Paul's concern for Onesimus even overshadows "the whole of Colossians" (*Philemon among the Letters,* 35), especially the *Haustafel* of Col 3:18–4:1, which "reflects the concrete facts of Onesimus' case" (ibid., 40; cf. 44). That, however, is clearly an exaggeration, as R. P. Martin has rightly shown (*Colossians and Philemon,* 147).

Although many modern interpreters maintain that the Epistle to the Colossians is Deutero-Pauline (i.e. written by a disciple of Paul who was well acquainted with his teaching), that view is not seen to affect the authenticity of the Letter to Philemon. If anything, the relationship of the two letters may even support the Pauline authorship of the Epistle to the Colossians, as a number of modern interpreters have argued (e.g. Knox, *Philemon among the Letters,* 34–55; Kümmel, *Introduction,* 345; Reicke, "Caesarea, Rome").

(8) Date and Place of Composition

Paul says that he writes this letter from prison (vv 1, 9–10, 13, 22–23), but it is almost impossible to say where he was then imprisoned. One can only speculate, and the speculation has been of three sorts.

(9) The traditional view (e.g. that of John Chrysostom, Jerome, H. Grotius) understands the imprisonment to be Paul's house-arrest in Rome, which is mentioned by Luke in Acts 28:16, 30. The Marcionite prologue reads: *Philemoni familiares literas facit pro Onesimo servo eius. Scribit autem ei a Roma de carcere* (He composes a private[?] letter to Philemon on behalf of Onesimus his servant, but he writes to him from prison in Rome [see D. de Bruyne, "Prologues bibliques d'origine marcionite," *RevBén* 24 (1907) 1–16]). This view is held also in modern times by Benoit, Bieder, Bruce, Cadoux, Caird, Dodd, Getty, Gülzow, Johnston, Lightfoot, Moule, Müller, O'Brien, Oesterley, Percy, Peretto, Schnelle, Scott, and Vincent. The distance between Rome and Colossae would have meant a lengthy sea voyage or, less likely, an arduous

journey over land most of the way for Onesimus, who has come to Paul in prison; but the prominence of Rome and its cosmopolitan character would have offered better cover for a slave. If this place of composition is correct, it would mean that the Letter to Philemon was written roughly A.D. 61–63, during the two years of Paul's detention in the capital of the Roman empire.

(10) Some commentators, however, prefer to ascribe the letter to Paul's imprisonment by the Roman authorities of Judea, when he was confined at Caesarea Maritima, which is also mentioned by Luke in Acts 23:35; 24:26–27. So Dibelius, Goguel, Greeven, Haupt, Lohmeyer, Oesterley (as an alternative), Reicke, and de Zwaan. Caesarea Maritima has the advantage of being closer to the town from which Onesimus comes than Rome, and it would involve a less arduous journey. If this place of composition is used, it would mean that the Letter to Philemon was written roughly A.D. 58–60. This view is only rarely espoused today.

(11) Still other commentators have argued for an imprisonment of Paul at Ephesus, which they infer from such passages in Paul's own letters as 1 Cor 15:32; 16:9; 2 Cor 1:8–9; 6:5; 11:23–24; Rom 16:7, in which he writes cryptically about some ordeal that he faced in Ephesus. So Binder, Deissmann, Duncan, Egger, Ernst, Friedrich, Gnilka, Harrison, Klijn, Knox, Lohse, Martin, Marxsen, Michaelis, Stuhlmacher, Vielhauer, Winter, Wolter, et al.

The Letter to Philemon perhaps could be related to the imprisonment about which Paul speaks in Phil 1:7, 12–13, 20–26, a letter in which Timothy is likewise a cosender, which most of the same interpreters relate to Ephesus. Reicke, however, argues strongly that the place from which Philippians was written is quite different from that of the other Letters of Captivity ("Caesarea, Rome").

In any case, about an Ephesian imprisonment of Paul Luke says nothing in Acts, not even at the time of the riot of the Ephesian silversmiths (Acts 19:21–40), where one might expect such a mention. However, the Marcionite Prologue to the Epistle to the Colossians states: *Apostolus iam ligatus scribit eis ab Epheso* (the Apostle already in bonds writes to them from Ephesus; see E. Preuschen, *Analecta,* 87). So Ephesus as a place of Pauline imprisonment is not a modern concoction. The connection of the Letter to Philemon to the Epistle to the Colossians mentioned above (§7) is invoked by some interpreters to support the Ephesian imprisonment from which Paul writes to Philemon, but that claim may be far from certain, as already indicated. If Ephesus is indeed the place where the Letter to Philemon was composed, then it was written roughly about A.D. 55–57, sometime during Paul's rather lengthy ministry in that important city in Asia Minor.

(12) The last view has the advantage of keeping Philemon (in Colossae) and Paul (in Ephesus) within a plausible distance (about 168 km, a distance that could be covered on foot in about a week). It would also explain more

easily Paul's plan to visit Philemon (v 22) once he is released from his imprisonment. The planned visit has always been seen as a major difficulty for the Roman hypothesis (but less of one for the Caesarean hypothesis), because one would have to explain how Onesimus, if he were a runaway slave, could have traveled so far without being discovered by some authorities and at such an expense. Dodd, however, once argued that it was just "as likely that the fugitive slave, his pockets lined at his master's expense, made for Rome *because* it was distant, as that he went to Ephesus because it was near" (*New Testament Studies*, 95).

(13) In any case, although I prefer Ephesus as the place of composition, that locale remains problematic, being only inferred from the Pauline passages noted above. As Dunn has noted, "it is difficult to come to any final decision. Fortunately, however, the exposition of the letter depends only marginally on the conclusion regarding its place of writing, so that to that extent the issue can be left open" (*Colossians and Philemon*, 308). If the Epistle to the Colossians is held to be Deutero-Pauline, then it would have been written about fifteen years later than this letter, and one would have to read it as a post-Philemon composition, not one written at the same time, as some modern commentators have contended (Knox).

II. Philemon, Onesimus, the Occasion and Purpose of the Letter

◆

(14) This Letter to Philemon is the shortest in the Pauline corpus, and yet it involves a story that is far bigger than it, because it stems from the imprisoned Apostle and concerns an issue of broad social concern in the ancient world in which he lived, the relation of a slave to his master. In order to understand the letter, one has to try to comprehend the story behind the writing. This narrative aspect of the letter and its relation to the social and economic world that it reflects have been well studied by N. R. Petersen in *Rediscovering Paul: Philemon and the Sociology of Paul's Narrative World.*

(15) Philemon

The one whose name this Pauline letter has traditionally borne and the main recipient of it was Philemon, a young, well-to-do, and respected Christian of a small Phrygian town in the Lycus Valley of Asia Minor. Verses 17–18 of the letter may imply that Philemon was a successful businessman, who traveled much and met Paul in the course of his travels, and even that Paul was his "partner" in such business. So Dunn would have it, and he may well be right (*Colossians and Philemon*, 301).

Philemon was probably a citizen of Colossae in Asia Minor. Onesimus, who is mentioned in v 10 of this letter, is said in the Epistle to the Colossians to be "one of yourselves" (Col 4:9) and to be traveling with Tychicus, who is making his way to Colossae (Col 4:7–9). Moreover, Archippus, one of the addressees of the Letter to Philemon, is actually given instructions in Col 4:17. Hence it would seem that he and Philemon both were residents of the town of Colossae and that from Philemon's house in that town Onesimus had come to where Paul was imprisoned. Being a Phrygian, Philemon was probably not a Roman citizen, but was governed indirectly by Roman law, seeing that the Romans controlled most of the towns of Asia Minor in the first century A.D. Since Philemon is the first named among the addressees and the singular "you" that is found in the bulk of the letter refers to him, he must be regarded as the master of the slave Onesimus, who is the object of Paul's correspondence with Philemon, *pace* L. Cope ("On Rethinking," 46), as Lohse rightly recognizes (*Colossians and Philemon*, 186).

(16) Philemon seems to have been converted by Paul. That is usually taken to be the implication of Paul's words when he says in v 19c, "you owe me even your own self." Philemon had met Paul somewhere, probably in Ephesus, where Paul exercised a considerable ministry (roughly A.D. 54–57). Thus Paul had become his spiritual father and Christian mentor. Philemon owned a number of slaves and a house large enough to accommodate the Christians of the town, who gathered in it for their liturgical services and common social activities (v 2). One might be inclined to think that Philemon had been a harsh taskmaster who gave Onesimus cause to come and seek Paul's intervention on his behalf, but Paul's letter gives no indication of anything like that and corrects any such conclusion that one might draw from Onesimus' departure.

(17) Schenk (*ANRW*, 3482–83), however, thinks that Philemon, a former persecutor of Christians, but now converted, actually lived in Pergamum, a different town in Asia Minor, because he sees a connection between v 22 (Paul's request that a guest-room be prepared for him when he is released from detention) and 2 Cor 1:8 and 2:12. That, however, is a far-fetched view, which has little basis in the Letter to Philemon itself. Moreover Pergamum is not mentioned in either passage of 2 Corinthians, nor even in the whole NT, save in the Book of Revelation (2:12); see further Dunn, *Colossians and Philemon*, 300 n. 2.

(18) Onesimus

This is the male slave who has come from Colossae to where Paul is imprisoned. We are not told how Onesimus and Paul have met. Again, one can only speculate: it might have been by chance; it might have been that he sought out Paul in his hunger or need; it might have been that Onesimus had heard his master Philemon speak about Paul, and so he was seeking his aid. It is often said that he may have been apprehended by authorities or caught in some criminal deed and came to be imprisoned in the same place where Paul was, but that is highly unlikely. If Onesimus had been so apprehended, he would have been confined in a prison for slaves (*ergastulum;* see Seneca, *De ira* 3.32), and scarcely in the same place as Paul, who seems to have been in *custodia libera* (liberal detention), something like the house-arrest that is mentioned in Acts 28:16, 30. It seems rather that Onesimus had not been arrested and was able to approach Paul easily. He must have been an educated slave, someone whom Paul would have preferred to keep with him rather than send back to his master.

(19) If Philemon had indeed been converted to Christianity through the instrumentality of Paul, he apparently did not see to it that all in his household became Christians. When Onesimus and Paul first met, Onesimus was still a pagan. Somehow Paul, even though imprisoned, managed to give Onesimus his attention, sought to help him, and ultimately converted him to Christianity ("whose father I have become in my imprisonment," v 10; see E. R. Goodenough, *HTR* 22 [1929] 181–83). Gnilka (*Philemonbrief*, 3) thinks that Onesimus met Paul before the latter was imprisoned, but that contradicts what Paul himself says in v 10. In any case, in the probably later letter to the Colossians, Onesimus is said to be returning to Colossae as "a faithful and beloved brother" (4:9) in the company of Tychicus (4:7). That seems to mean that Onesimus had been sent by Philemon to work with Paul, as he had implicitly requested (v 13), sometime after Paul had written this letter on his behalf to his master Philemon.

(20) Knox (*Philemon among the Letters*) maintained that Onesimus was the slave, not of Philemon, but of Archippus, who is mentioned among the addressees of the Letter to Philemon, as well as in Col 4:17. According to Knox, it is far from certain that Onesimus was a runaway slave, as he has been understood traditionally, or that Paul was appealing to Philemon on his behalf that he might be welcomed back without punishment (p. 18). *Parakalō se peri tou emou teknou* (v 10) would mean, "I appeal to you for my child," i.e. Paul was simply asking *for* Onesimus: "with all possible delicacy . . . asserting a claim upon Onesimus" (p. 24). Moreover Onesimus has been separated from his master for a little while "in order that he might thenceforth possess him *not as a slave*, but in a quite new sense, *forever*. Onesimus has now become his brother in Christ" (p. 27). Knox claims that he is following Theophylact, Jülicher, and Lohmeyer in thus understanding Paul's request for Onesimus. Furthermore Knox insists on the relation of the Letter to Philemon and the Epistle to the Colossians "in the closest possible fashion" (p. 55), both being written by Paul "about the same time." In Col 4:16c Paul refers to another missive described as *tēn ek Laodikeias*, "the (letter) from Laodicea," which, as K. G. Wieseler and E. J. Goodspeed had noted, is the Letter to Philemon. In the following verse (4:17) Paul urges the Colossians to see that Archippus (also mentioned in Phlm 2) fulfills his *diakonia*. Archippus and Onesimus were both Colossians (Col 4:9, 17), resident in Colossae. The Letter to Philemon gives no directive to forward it to Colossae (p. 49), in contradistinction to the directive in Col 4:16c. If Paul were sending it to Colossae, it would come there "from Laodicea" (p. 55), where Philemon resides. Archippus and Onesimus are mentioned in the Letter to Philemon and the Epistle to the Colossians, and in the latter the letter "from Laodicea" is closely connected with Archip-

pus. The *diakonia* that Archippus is to fulfill is none other than the main concern of the Letter to Philemon, among the addressees of which is Archippus (v 2). "A slaveowner is asked to give up a slave for Christian service" (pp. 57–58, 69); note especially the occurrence of the verb *diakonein* in Phlm 13. "This clearly points to Archippus' being the owner of the slave" (p. 58); and at his house in Colossae the church met (v 2). Onesimus carries the letter, but "Paul is troubled because he does not know Onesimus' master" (p. 63); that is why he includes the church among the addressees. Whereas Archippus was a Colossian, Philemon was "a Laodicean" (p. 70), and Laodicea was the natural place of his residence. Paul's letter was directed first to Philemon in Laodicea, who was expected to use his influence with Archippus of Colossae and see that both it and Onesimus reached Archippus and the church that met at his house. Archippus would, then, be the real, intended recipient of the Letter to Philemon. For Knox, Onesimus would have returned subsequently to Paul as a helper in his evangelization, would have eventually become the bishop of Ephesus (see Ignatius of Antioch, *Eph.* 1:3; cf. 2:1; 6:2), and would have played a major role in collecting Paul's letters into a corpus, having been the person about whom the Letter to Philemon was written (pp. 103, 107). In this view, Knox is followed by L. Cope, J. E. Jones, J. L. Houlden, and S. B. C. Winter.

(21) The last three suggestions of Knox may have some plausibility. That Onesimus became a bishop of Ephesus is a possibility—no more than that—which had already been proposed by a number of commentators ever since the time of John Chrysostom (e.g. Goodspeed, Harrison, Moule). Others, however, think that such an identification is "mere speculation" because of "the frequent occurrence of the name [Onesimus]" in ancient documents and inscriptions (Marxsen, *Introduction*, 70; similarly Stuhlmacher, *Brief an Philemon*, 18). Since Ignatius wrote ca. A.D. 110, almost fifty years after Paul wrote this letter about Onesimus, and since Ignatius seems to have been speaking about a relatively young bishop in *Eph.* 1–3, it may indeed be another Onesimus about whom he writes. See further J. W. Martens, who has refuted Knox's position about the relation of Paul's Onesimus to that of Ignatius' letter to the Ephesians ("Ignatius and Onesimus"). It has also been claimed that Onesimus became a bishop rather of Beroea in Macedonia, as *Apostolic Constitutions* 7.46 seems to suggest.

Because the Letter to Philemon has been included in the Pauline corpus and because it deals with a matter that is quite personal to Paul, Mitton agrees that this is a good reason to regard Onesimus as having been involved in the gathering of letters that make up the Pauline corpus. Otherwise it is hard to explain why this letter is found in that corpus. Similarly Stuhlmacher, *Brief an Philemon*, 18; Bruce, *The Epistles*, 200–2.

(22) Nevertheless, the main contentions of Knox's interpretation are quite tenuous. Much of his theory depends on whether the Letter to Philemon and

the Epistle to the Colossians were written about the same time. They may be "at least 15 years apart," as Gnilka notes (*Philemonbrief*, 5). According to Col 4:9, Onesimus was a "faithful and beloved brother," a Colossian, who was accompanying Tychicus to Colossae. If the Epistle to the Colossians is a Deutero-Pauline composition, then it must have been composed at a time later than what is being said in Phlm 10–11. Hence the Letter to Philemon could scarcely have been carried by Tychicus, as perhaps might be implied by Col 4:9, and as some other commentators have also interpreted that verse (e.g. Grotius, Preiss; Dibelius, *An Philemon*, 105). That some phrases in this letter echo those of Colossians is clear, but such echoes do not warrant the synchronizing of them temporally, as Knox would have it. It may be rather the other way round: that the later Epistle to the Colossians echoes phrases in this Pauline letter because of its dependence on it.

(23) Moreover there is not the slightest hint in the Letter to Philemon that would identify it as the "letter from Laodicea" (Col 4:16c), despite the suggestion of Goodspeed that Knox adopts. If the Letter to Philemon were meant there, why would it be called *tēn ek Laodikeias*, "the one from Laodicea"? Knox's explanation of the preposition *ek* is forced and far-fetched. If Marcion later knew of both the Letter to Philemon and an Epistle to the Laodiceans (equaling what we normally call the Epistle to the Ephesians), that would argue for a difference between them.

(24) Any ordinary reading of Phlm 1–4 would note that Philemon, the first-named addressee, is considered the master of Onesimus and that the singular "you" in vv 2, 4 refers to Philemon, who is resident in the same town as that from which Onesimus has come. Would Paul write for Onesimus in such subtle delicacy in this letter, only to pressure Archippus himself (by name) in a separate, public letter (addressed to the Christians of Colossae) with the instruction to fulfill the "ministry received in the Lord," if that meant the emancipation of Onesimus, as Knox's theory maintains? That seems hardly likely. Furthermore v 19c, "you owe me even your own self," goes unexplained in Knox's interpretation. This is usually interpreted to mean that Paul was instrumental in the conversion of Onesimus' master, but when Archippus is said to be his master and unknown to Paul, that part of v 19 creates a considerable difficulty.

As Lohse has put it (*Colossians and Philemon*, 187),

> Knox's hypothesis collapses when one enforces the methodological rule of first trying to understand a writing in the light of its own statements before drawing on other documents for purposes of comparison. The letter to Philemon itself offers no basis whatsoever for the position that Archippus, not Philemon, was the recipient of the letter.

See further the critiques of Benoit, "Philémon," 1206; Bruce, *BJRL* 48 (1965–66) 91–96; Greeven, "Prüfung," 373–78; Harrison, "Onesimus," 268–94; Kümmel, *Introduction*, 349; O'Brien, *Introductory Thanksgivings*, 48 n. 4; Schmauch, *EKL*, 3. 183.

Finally, Harrison speculates that Onesimus "is the same person as Onesiphorus" of 2 Tim 1:16–18 ("Onesimus," 288, 293), but that does not seem very likely, because they are two very different names.

(25) Occasion

Four explanations have been given for what occasioned Paul's writing the Letter to Philemon.

(a) The traditional explanation has been that the slave Onesimus had run away from Philemon's house and become *phygas* or *drapetēs* or *fugitivus*, "fugitive," perhaps after having caused his master considerable damage (vv 11, 18). Lightfoot thought that the slave had stolen something, as did the proverbial runaway slave in Roman comedies (see Terence, *Phormio* 1.4.11–13): he "had 'packed up some goods and taken to his heels' " (*Colossians and Philemon*, 310). He came to where Paul was imprisoned, perhaps because he knew how his master Philemon esteemed Paul, or because he was brought by one of Paul's associates who found him in his flight (e.g. Epaphras, the evangelist of the Lycus Valley [Col 1:7]), or because he was seeking asylum in the place where Paul was. For any such reason, Onesimus as a runaway has come to where Paul is.

So most older commentators from the time of John Chrysostom on have explained Onesimus' situation, even though Paul nowhere says in the letter that Onesimus "has run away." Among modern interpreters, J. M. G. Barclay, Caird, Collange, Fitzmyer (in *JBC* and *NJBC*), Getty, Harrison, Llewelyn, Lightfoot, Michaelis, Martin, Nordling, O'Brien, Peretto, Petersen, Robertson, Saunders, Soards, Stuhlmacher, Suhl have so understood the situation.

(b) Another explanation of the occasion of Paul's writing this letter is that Onesimus comes merely as a messenger sent to Paul by his owner with a message or a gift for the imprisoned Paul (Knox) or as one "*sent* by the congregation in Colossae" to bring Paul "food and services" (Winter, "Paul's Letter," 3). Paul would be writing, then, to ask for Onesimus, that he be released from his obligations in Colossae so that he might come to help Paul in evangelization, because as a Christian he should not be considered a slave in a Christian community and should be emancipated. Similarly R. E. Glaze, "Onesimus"; C. S. Wansink, *Chained in Christ*, 147–99.

(c) Still another explanation maintains that Paul, who never uses the technical term *phygas* or *drapetēs* in his letter and does not tell us why Onesimus decided to leave Colossae, writes this letter on behalf of Onesimus, who is not a runaway slave, but rather a slave who has been in some domestic trouble with his master Philemon and who has come to seek the intervention of an *amicus domini* (friend of the master) in the hope that he might be restored peacefully to his former status in the master's household. Thus Onesimus would have risked traveling alone as a slave and coming to Paul, his master's Christian mentor, so that he as *amicus domini* could act as an intermediary and exert his religious influence over Philemon. This explanation is similar to that of Knox and Winter in maintaining that Onesimus was not *fugitivus*, but differs in explaining the reason why Onesimus has sought Paul's intercession. It is based largely on ancient extrabiblical testimonies about slaves and has been proposed by Lampe and seconded by Rapske. It is preferred by Bartchy, Dunn, Patzia.

(d) Another more recent explanation, put forth by A. D. Callahan, maintains that Onesimus was not a slave at all, but rather a "brother" of Philemon, "both in the consanguinary sense *(en sarki)* and the religious sense *(en kyriō)*" ("Paul's Epistle to Philemon," 370). "In this short, diplomatic epistle Paul attempted deftly to heal a rift not between errant slave and irate master, but between estranged Christian brothers" (p. 371). "Nothing in the text conclusively indicates that Onesimus was ever the chattel of the letter's chief addressee" (p. 362). "The problem that Paul engaged in the letter was not that Onesimus was a real slave (for he was not), nor that Onesimus was not a real brother to Philemon (for he was), but that Onesimus was not a *beloved* brother to Philemon. The emphasis of verse 16b, therefore, is not on *adelphon*, but on *agapēton*" (p. 372). Moreover Callahan maintains that the intepretation of Onesimus as a runaway slave was unknown in the early church prior to John Chrysostom, who speculated and introduced this "imaginative and ingenious hypothesis" (p. 368), and his understanding of the situation has thus misled countless subsequent interpreters. In part, then, Callahan agrees with Knox, Lampe, and others that there is no mention of Onesimus as a runaway slave in the letter; but he presses further and maintains that there is no mention even of Onesimus as a slave, for he was Philemon's blood brother.

(26) It is not easy to decide which of these opinions explains best the occasion of the writing of the Letter to Philemon. Although I once followed the traditional explanation (a), I now realize that there is much to be said for the third view (c), which I am adopting here, for reasons to be explained below (§30–34).

The second explanation (b) is inadequate, because it glosses over too much of the subtle argumentation of Paul's letter and scarcely explains why Onesimus, a "useless" pagan slave (v 11), would have been sent by Philemon or the Colossian congregation to help Paul. There are also other minor (grammatical) elements in Knox's and Winter's interpretations that are impossible or unlikely; they will be mentioned in the NOTES on the verses concerned. See further B. M. Rapske, "The Prisoner Paul"; Bartchy, *ABD*, 5. 307–8.

(27) The fourth explanation (d) is likewise inadequate, because it not only misinterprets John Chrysostom and other patristic writers, as Mitchell has rightly shown ("John Chrysostom on Philemon"), but offers a strained and impossible interpretation of several verses in the letter, esp. vv 15–16. Paul's words, *hina aiōnion auton apechēs, ouketi hōs doulon all' hyper doulon, adelphon agapēton,* "that you may have him back for ever, no longer as a slave but as more than a slave, as a beloved brother," cannot be twisted to mean, "that you may have him back forever, no longer as if he were a slave" (Callahan, "Paul's Epistle to Philemon," 373). The conjunction *hōs* cannot be given a contrary-to-fact nuance (see NOTE on v 16). Moreover, to call Philemon and Onesimus "estranged Christian brothers" (p. 371) contradicts the Pauline text itself about Onesimus becoming a Christian through the instrumentality of Paul the prisoner (v 10). That verse suggests that Onesimus must have been a pagan when he left Colossae to come to where Paul was. Although Callahan sought to answer Mitchell ("John Chrysostom on Philemon"), his reply merely repeats what he had already said in his first article, with little added that is substantially new. See further J. M. G. Barclay, *Colossians and Philemon,* 99.

(28) Part of Callahan's argument was based also on the interpretation of the Letter to Philemon among American antebellum abolitionists who advanced biblical arguments against slavery and maintained the dearth of evidence for the traditional interpretation of the Letter to Philemon. Whereas proslavery advocates appealed to the letter as "the Pauline Mandate" (see L. R. Morrison, "The Religious Defense," 19), abolitionists insisted that there was no evidence "that Onesimus was a slave," and claimed that he was "a natural brother of Philemon" (Callahan, "Paul's Epistle to Philemon," 363). See A. Barnes, *An Inquiry,* 321–22, who preferred to translate *doulos* as "servant" and argued that the Greek term was

> of a general character, and would be applied to *any one* who was engaged in the service of another, whether bound by a parent or guardian, or whether he engaged voluntarily to serve another, or whether he was purchased as a slave, or whether he was a *serf* attached to the soil. The word denotes *servant* of any kind, and it should never be assumed that those to whom it was applied were slaves.

For a similar approach, see G. Bourne, *A Condensed Anti-Slavery Bible Argument,* and J. G. Fee, *An Anti-Slavery Manual.*

(29) That, however, is a highly questionable interpretation of *doulos,* undoubtedly influenced by the then widely used KJV, which renders v 16, "Not now as a servant, but above a servant, a brother beloved, specially to me, but

how much more unto thee, both in the flesh, and in the Lord?" See further J. A. Harrill, *CBQ* 60 (1998) 757–59. Both the KJV's rendering of that and similar verses and the institution of slavery itself in the pre-Lincoln United States of America have conditioned countless American interpreters of the NT against the translation of *doulos* as "slave," a term, however, that would have been perfectly at home in the world of Paul of Tarsus. Compare K. Giles, "The Biblical Argument."

(30) The third explanation (c), which I now prefer, is based partly on a situation known from the first-century Roman jurist Proculus, who is quoted in Justinian's *Digest* (21.1.17.4; cf. 21.1.43.1), and partly on letters of Pliny the Younger to Sabinianus (*Ep.* 9.21 and 9.24).

(31) Proculus, a prominent Roman jurist of the first half of the first Christian century, about whom little is otherwise known, was often quoted by later jurists. An opinion of his about a runaway slave is quoted in Justinian's *Digest* 21.1.17.4 (ed. Mommsen, 2. 606); it runs as follows:

> *Idem [Vivianus] ait, interrogatus Proculus de eo, qui domi latuisset in hoc scilicet, ut fugae nactus occasionem se subtraheret, ait: tametsi fugere non posset videri, qui domi mansisset, tamen eum fugitivum fuisse: sin autem in hoc tantum latuisset, quoad iracundia domini effervesceret, fugitivum non esse, sicuti ne eum quidem, qui cum dominum animadverteret verberibus se adficere velle, praeripuisset se ad amicum, quem ad precandum perduceret.*

> The same [Vivian] says that, when Proculus was asked about one who had hidden at home in order to find an opportunity to escape, said: although he could not yet be seen to have run away, being still at home, he was nonetheless a fugitive; but if he had hidden only until his master's anger abated, he would not be a fugitive, just as the one who, when he realized that his master wanted to whip him, betook himself to a friend whom he induced to intercede for him.

From such an ancient Roman legal writer one has derived the notion of a slave's recourse to *amicus domini* (friend of the master) to get him to intervene on his behalf when he had incurred the wrath of his master over some detail. Although he betook himself to the place of the master's friend, he was not considered legally to be a runaway. See also the opinion of Vivianus himself about a slave who has fled to his mother to seek her aid and entreaties (*Digest* 21.1.17.5 [ed. Mommsen, 2. 606]); and the view of the third-century Julius Paulus: *Qui ad amicum domini deprecaturus confugit, non est fugitivus* (The slave who betakes himself to a friend of [his] master to seek his intervening is not a fugitive), *Digest* 21.1.43.1 (ed. Mommsen, 2. 618).

(32) C. Plinius Caecilius Secundus, or Pliny the Younger (A.D. 61–112), is

known from his writings and from various inscriptions. He would have been almost a contemporary of Paul in the Roman world and wrote a Latin letter to a certain Sabinianus (*Ep.* 9.21), which is also seen to be relevant to the interpretation of this Pauline letter:

C. *Plinius Sabiniano Suo S.*
Libertus tuus, cui succensere te dixeras, venit ad me, advolutusque pedibus meis, tamquam tuis haesit. Flevit multum, multumque rogavit, multum etiam tacuit; in summa, fecit mihi fidem poenitentiae. Vere credo emendatum, quia deliquisse se sentit.

Irasceris, scio; et irasceris merito, id quoque scio; sed tunc praecipua mansuetudinis laus, cum irae causa iustissima est. Amasti hominem et, spero, amabis; interim sufficit, ut exorari te sinas. Licebit rursus irasci, si meruerit, quod exoratus excusatius facies. Remitte aliquid adulescentiae ipsius, remitte lacrimis, remitte indulgentiae tuae; ne torseris illum, ne torseris etiam te. Torqueris enim, cum tam lenis irasceris.

Vereor, ne videar non rogare, sed cogere, si precibus eius meas iunxero. Iungam tamen tanto plenius et effusius, quanto ipsum acrius severiusque corripui destricte minatus numquam me postea rogaturum. Hoc illi, quem terreri oportebat, tibi non idem. Nam fortasse iterum rogabo, impetrabo iterum; sit modo tale, ut rogare me, ut praestare te deceat. Vale.

C. Pliny to Sabinianus, G(reetings).
Your freedman, whom you had mentioned as having displeased you, has come to me; he threw himself at my feet and clung to them as he could have to yours. He cried much, begged constantly, even with much silence; in short, he has convinced me that he repents of what he did. I truly believe that he is reformed, because he recognizes that he has been delinquent.

You are angry, I know, and rightly so, as I also recognize; but clemency wins the highest praise when the reason for anger is most righteous. You once had affection for (this) human being, and, I hope, you will have it again. Meanwhile it suffices that you let me prevail upon you. Should he again incur your displeasure, you will have so much more reason to be angry, as you give in now. Allow somewhat for his youth, for his tears, and for your own indulgent conduct. Do not antagonize him, lest you antagonize yourself at the same time; for when a man of your mildness is angry, you will be antagonizing yourself.

I fear that, in joining my entreaties to his, I may seem rather to compel than to request (you to forgive him). Nevertheless, I shall join them so much more fully and unreservedly, because I have sharply and severely reproved him, positively threatening never to entreat again on his behalf. Although I said this to him, who should become more fearful (of offending),

I do not say it to you. I may perhaps have occasion to entreat you again and obtain your forgiveness, but may it be such that it will be proper for me to intercede and you to pardon. Farewell.

Here we see Pliny acting as *amicus domini* in the case of a freedman, a slave who had been emancipated, but who still retained a relationship to his master. What is striking in this letter of Pliny, in which he intercedes on behalf of the delinquent freedman, is the mention of the latter's repentance and regret, a detail that is completely lacking in Paul's letter about Onesimus. Moreover there is also the explicit plea of Pliny that Sabinianus forgive the delinquent freedman. In this way the letter of Pliny differs from that of Paul. Paul's letter, however, is much more delicately composed and passes over with subtlety the bygone infidelity of Onesimus, which Paul does not deny. Even though Paul does not explicitly plead for Philemon's forgiveness, the general attitude of Paul's letter does so implicitly, especially when Paul writes, "welcome him as you would welcome me" (v 17).

(33) Moreover Pliny wrote again about the same matter (*Ep.* 9.24):

C. Plinius Sabiniano Suo S.
Bene fecisti, quod libertum tibi carum reducentibus epistulis meis in domum, in animum recepisti. Iuvabit hoc te; me certe iuvat, primum quod te tam tractabilem video, ut in ira regi possis, deinde quod tantum mihi tribuis, ut vel auctoritati meae pareas vel precibus indulgeas. Igitur et laudo et gratias ago; simul in posterum moneo, ut te erroribus tuorum, etsi non fuerit, quod deprecetur, placabilem praestes. Vale.

C. Pliny to Sabinianus, G(reetings).
You have done well, on the receipt of my letter, to welcome back into your house and your affection the freedman who was once so dear to you. This will help you greatly; it certainly helps me, first of all, when I see that you are pliant enough to be governed in your anger. Then too that you grant me so much, either in seeming to yield to my authority or in giving way to my entreaties. I praise you, then, and thank you; at the same time, I counsel you for the future that you show yourself tolerant of the mistakes of your (slaves), even if there be no one to intervene on their behalf. Farewell.

The second letter reveals that the entreaty Pliny had made on behalf of the freedman was successful. It seems to be similar to what the Epistle to the Colossians suggests: since Onesimus has been working with Paul, he seems to have become a freedman of Philemon by the time that that epistle was written. Compare S. K. Stowers, *Letter Writing in Greco-Roman Antiquity* (Philadelphia, Pa.: Westminster, 1986) 160. Thus the two letters of Pliny reveal the power that an *amicus domini* could have in interceding on behalf of a *libertus*, a slave who had been freed. The same kind of intercession would have been possible for a slave. This would be the kind of letter that Paul is writing on behalf of Onesimus to Philemon.

(34) Furthermore an incident in the life of the emperor Caesar Augustus, recounted by the Roman historian Dio Cassius (*Rom. Hist.* 54.23.2–5) and L. Annaeus Seneca of Corduba (*De ira* 3.40.2–4), illustrates the kind of intervention that an *amicus domini* could make with the master of a slave. In this case, it is not a letter written on behalf of a slave, but the good word of one who knew the master. Augustus was dining once with Vedius Pollio when one of the latter's slaves broke a crystal goblet. Pollio cruelly ordered him to be seized and thrown to man-eating lampreys that he kept in a pond on his estate. The lad slipped from his captors and fled to Augustus' feet, begging only that he might die some other way. Caesar Augustus ordered the lad to be pardoned, that all the other crystal goblets in the house be brought and broken in his presence, and that the pond be filled up. So Augustus intervened on behalf of a slave and acted as a sort of *amicus domini.*

These, then, are the reasons that make the third explanation (c) of the occasion of the writing of the Letter to Philemon the more likely one, but one cannot gloss over the differences in the case of Onesimus pointed out above. For further minor objections against this explanation, see S. R. Llewelyn, *NDIEC* 8 (1997–98) 40–46.

(35) Purpose

No matter what the occasion of the Letter to Philemon might have been, it is clear that Paul writes a personal and closely argued letter on behalf of Onesimus, who he has come to learn was a slave of Philemon. Paul writes, indeed, with utmost delicacy as *amicus domini* for Onesimus, who has sought his intercession. Although Paul would have liked to retain Onesimus for his work of evangelization, he recognizes Philemon's legal right and has decided to send Onesimus back to him (vv 14, 16). Paul diplomatically intercedes in a difficult concrete situation with Philemon on behalf of Onesimus. Instead of trying to exert his apostolic authority, he pleads with Philemon to take Onesimus back "no longer as a slave but . . . as a beloved brother" (v 16), even to welcome him as he would welcome Paul himself. Paul counsels Philemon to act in this matter "out of love" (v 9). In effect, with subtle rhetoric and pressure, Paul implicitly asks Philemon not to inflict on Onesimus the penalties permitted by law and promises to restore any damage that Onesimus may have caused. In v 21 Paul goes even further and pleads with Philemon to do "even more than I ask."

The letter does not purport to be a Pauline declaration about the institution of slavery; it differs notably from the regulations for slaves laid down in Col 3:22–4:1 and Eph 6:5–9, and even from what Paul himself wrote in 1 Cor 7:20–24. Rather, the Apostle has won Onesimus over to Christian faith and now appeals on his behalf with his Christian master Philemon of Colossae. He thus intercedes to obtain for Onesimus an assured return to his master's house in the status of a slave, and also as a Christian, "as more than a slave, as a beloved brother" (v 16).

Paul further suggests that he would like to have Onesimus come back to work with him in the evangelization of the area where Paul is imprisoned (v 20), but he is willing to forgo that benefit, if only Philemon will forget the past. Paul guarantees Philemon that he will go bond for the financial loss that Onesimus has caused him. Thus Paul seeks to get both Philemon and the Colossian congregation that meets at his house to treat Onesimus with faith, hope, and joy, welcoming him even at their celebration of the Lord's Supper.

Paul may be implying that Philemon should emancipate Onesimus, but that is never expressly stated. The question of how Philemon should deal with Onesimus in the near future is left to Philemon. Paul desires only that his decision be made out of love. Paul's letter is a petition, one motivated by love for a fellow Christian.

The Epistle to the Colossians seems to show that Paul's Letter to Philemon achieved its purpose, because it reveals that Philemon did the "more" at which Paul hinted: he set Onesimus free to become a coworker of Paul.

(36) Possibly this letter was carried by Onesimus himself, and so it may seem to have been intended by Paul to be like a letter of recommendation for Onesimus, but it is actually a petitionary letter (*Bittschrift*). It may be related to letters of recommendation, such as Paul writes elsewhere (Rom 16:1–3 [for Phoebe]; 1 Cor 16:10–11 [for Timothy]; 2 Cor 8:22–23 [for an unnamed "brother"]), but that is only a superficial resemblance, for it is really more, as the comparision with the letters of Pliny shows.

III. Slavery in Antiquity

◆

(37) Slavery

Webster's Third New International Dictionary defines a slave as "a person held in servitude: one that is the chattel of another," i.e. a human being held in bondage by another and subjected to compulsory work and dependency, which sometimes amounted to inhuman exploitation. In the ancient world the condition of a *doulos* or *servus* (male) or *doulē* or *serva* (female) was not always regarded as inhuman or degrading, for slavery formed a normal part of many societies and cultures and was an integral part of their economic structures. Along with husbands, wives, sons, and daughters, male and female slaves were components of the *familia* in the Roman world and of the *patria* in the Greek world. This can be seen clearly from the Pauline corpus itself: in Col 3:18–4:1 and Eph 5:22–6:9—as well as in 1 Pet 2:18–3:7—in which counsels for the conduct of members of the "family" are spelled out, and they include "slaves" explicitly. In such ancient societies and cultures all depended on the master's treatment of the slaves he owned, and in the majority of instances slaves were well treated. See further S. S. Bartchy, *Mallon chrēsai,* 37–87; R. Gayer, *Die Stellung,* 275–82; W. L. Westermann, *Slave Systems.*

(38) In ancient Roman society, slavery (*servitus*) was recognized as an institution of *ius gentium* (law of the clans); it involved a person, *servus* or *serva,* who *domino alieno contra naturam subicitur* (against nature is subjected to the ownership of another; *Digest* 1.5.4.1 [ed. Mommsen, 1. 15]). *Servile caput nullum ius habet* (a slave has no rights; *Digest* 4.5.3.1 [ed. Mommsen, 1. 139]). The idea of a person who belonged to another as property or chattel was essential to slavery, but various degrees of ownership were often admitted; the degrees also stipulated relationships that existed between slaves and masters in a complex world. The maximum was one of hostility, and a Roman proverb conveyed it: *Totidem hostes esse quot servos* (There are as many enemies as there are slaves). See further Seneca, *Epistulae morales* 47.

Because of debts, a person could sell himself into slavery to another. Captives in war and those kidnapped by pirates often became slaves of their captors. Such slaves were bought, sold, rented out, or lent to another master, and their lives were characterized as "work, punishment, and food" (Pseudo-

Aristotle, *Oec.* 1344a 35). The *servus fidelis* (faithful slave) was often rewarded with manumission, which also occurred at the death of a master. He then became *libertus*, "freedman," but was often still related to the master, who was his *patronus*. The lazy, careless, or destructive slave, however, was often subject to severe punishment from his master. Wealthy Roman landlords often possessed thousands of slaves.

(39) In the contemporary Greek world, the slave was *doulos* or *doulē*, and his or her condition was called *douleia*. Aristotle defined the slave as *ktēma ti empsychon*, "an ensouled piece of property" (*Politics* 1.2 §1253b), who belongs wholly to his master (1.2 §1254a). Slaves were often well educated and were entrusted with the supervision and training of free sons and daughters of the family. They performed a variety of tasks in the society in which they lived; some were administrators of estates, household managers, and foremen of laborers, but others were retained for more menial tasks. A census taken up in Athens and reported by Demetrius of Phalerum in 309 B.C. numbered 21,000 citizens, 10,000 resident aliens, and is usually said to have counted 400,000 slaves. The last figure has been shown to be inflated, but the number of slaves was more likely the equivalent of both citizens and resident aliens. See W. S. Ferguson, *Hellenistic Athens* (London: Macmillan, 1911) 54. It has been estimated that in general about a third of the ancient population in Greece and Italy would have been slaves.

(40) Flight from Slavery

The running away of slaves was feared much by slave owners and was regulated in the Greco-Roman world by varied legislation. The technical expression for a runaway slave was *phygas* or *drapetēs* in Greek and *fugitivus* in Latin, "a fugitive." When a slave became a fugitive, he committed a serious crime, and his owner could take out a warrant against him.

Such a warrant, dating from the mid-second century B.C., is preserved in *P. Parisiensis* 10 (see U. Wilcken, *Urkunden der Ptolemäerzeit* [2 vols.; Berlin and Leipzig: de Gruyter, 1927, 1957], 1. §121, pp. 566–76, esp. 573–74). It runs:

Tou 25 Epeiph 16. Aristogenou tou Chrysippou
Alabandeōs presbeutou pais anekechō-
rēken (2) *en Alexandreiāi,* (1) *hōi onoma Hermōn, hos kai Neilos*
kaleitai, to genos Syros apo Bambykēs,
hōs etōn 18, megethei mesos, ageneios
euknēmos koilogeneios, phakos para rina
ex aristerōn, oulē hyper chalinon ex aristerōn
estigmenos ton dexion karpon grammasi

barbarikois dysin, echōn chrysiou episēmou
mnaieia 3, *pinas* 10, *krikon sidēroun,*
en hōi lēkythos kai xystrai, kai peri to sōma
chlamyda kai perizōma. Touton hos an ana-
gagē, lēpsetai chalkou 2 (2) 3, (1) *eph' hierou deixas* 1 (2) 2
(1) *par' andri axiochreiōi kai dōsidikōi* 3 (2) 5.
(1) *Mēnyein de ton boulomenon tois para tou*
stratēgou.
Estin de kai ho synapodedrakōs autōi
Biōn doulos Kallikratou tōn peri aulēn
archypēretōn, megethei brachys, platys
apo tōn ōmōn, kataknēmos, charopos,
hos kai echōn anakechōrēken himation kai
himatidion paidariou kai sebition gynai-
keion axion 6 *kai chalkou* * * 5.
touton hos an anag<ag>ēi lēpsetai hosa kai hyper tou
progegrammenou. Mēnyein de kai hyper
toutou tois para tou stratēgou.

N.B. (2) precedes words or figures added by a second hand; (1) denotes the resumption of the original text.

The (year) 25, Epiph 16. The slave of Aristogenes, son of Chrysippus, ambassador of Alabanda, has run away (in Alexandria). His name is Hermon, also called Nilus; a Syrian, by birth, from Bambyke [= Hierapolis]. His age is about 18, of medium height, clean-shaven, sturdy of leg, with a dimple in the chin, a mole to the left of the nose, a scar above the mouth to the left, branded on the right wrist with two foreign letters. He has 3 minas of coined gold, 10 pearls, an iron ring, on which are a flask and scrapers. He is wearing a cloak and an undergarment. Whoever brings him back will receive 2 (3) bronze (talents); (whoever does so by) indicating the shrine (where he has taken asylum), 1 (2) (talent[s]); (whoever does so by indicating that he is) with an important person subject to the law, 3 (5) (talents). (Whoever) wishes to give information should do so to the governor's agents.

There is also Bion, the slave of Callicrates, one of the chief officers at court, who has run away with him [i.e. with Hermon]. He is short in height, broad-shouldered, thin(?), with blue-gray eyes. He has run away with a coat, a child's short coat, and a woman's box worth 6 (talents) and 5* * (drachmas). Whoever bri<ng>s him back will receive the same as for the aforesaid. To give information about him, (report) to the governor's agents.

Such a public notice was posted in parts of Egypt, even outside of Alexandria; hence the secondary modification of the text. It shows that a slave named

Hermon and his companion Bion had run away from their master Aristogenes. Hermon is described as a Syrian from Bambyke, eighteen years old and of medium height; he wears an undergarment and a cloak and has three gold coins, ten pearls, and an iron ring. A reward is offered to whoever might apprehend him and bring him back or might reveal where he has taken asylum; such a person should report to the governor's office. Similar details describe Bion. See further other texts collected by S. R. Llewelyn in "The Government's Pursuit of Runaway Slaves," *NDIEC* 8 (1997–98) 9–46; cf. P. Arzt, "Brauchbare Sklaven."

(41) Runaway slaves often sought asylum in a shrine, sanctuary, or even the hearth of a family in the contemporary Greco-Roman world (e.g. in the Artemision of Ephesus [see Euripides, *Suppliants* 267; Philo, *De virtutibus* 24 §124]), or they could try to lose themselves in the subculture of a big city, where they might eke out their existence as beggars, thieves, or prostitutes (Epictetus, *Dissertationes* 1.29.59–61; 4.1.33–36), or they might join bands of robbers, or they might flee to a foreign land (Pliny, *Ep.* 10.74) and find work in an area where there was a shortage of laborers, especially in an agrarian district such as southern Italy. See further W. L. Westermann, *Slave Systems,* 40–41, 90–92, 126–28.

(42) If a runaway slave was discovered by someone, that person was obligated to notify the nearest municipal magistrate (*Digest* 11.4.1.1–6 [ed. Mommsen, 1. 344–45]). Lawful authorities could return him to his master, and he would be recommitted to his service. An ancient papyrus letter (*P. Lugd. Bat.* XX.36 [= *P. Mich. Zen.* 18]) tells of a slave named Stachys, who was apprehended by a certain Menes, taken to a house of Amyntas, and handed over to be with the other slaves (see S. R. Llewelyn, *NDIEC* 6 [1992] 57–60).

That was the least that the runaway might expect, because he was liable to far greater punishment. Severe penalties were permitted by law to be carried out against a runaway slave: he could be sold by his master to another, perhaps harsher slave owner; he could be scourged, branded, mutilated, or fitted with a metal collar, perhaps even be crucified, thrown to beasts, or killed (see *P. Oxy.* 14. 1643 [dated A.D. 298], which instructs a friend of the master of a runaway slave to go to Alexandria and apprehend the slave, who is known to him; he is to imprison him, flog him, and indict those who have harbored the slave; also *P. Oxy.* 12. 1423 [4th century A.D.]). See further Coleman-Norton, "The Apostle Paul," 174–77; Gnilka, *Philemonbrief*, 54–81; Nordling, "Onesimus Fugitivus," 114–17.

(43) To harbor a slave was a crime (*P. Oxy.* 12. 1422; *Digest* 11.4.1.1 [ed. Mommsen, 1. 344]), because it involved *furtum* (theft) of the property of another.

There was, however, a lucrative trade in antiquity for those who helped runaway slaves either to be resold to a more benign master or to be emancipated; see D. Daube, "Dodges and Rackets in Roman Law," *Proceedings of the Classical Association* 61 (1964) 28–30; cf. Nordling, "Onesimus Fugitivus," 104.

(44) SLAVERY IN JUDAISM

The ancient Hebrews as a people knew slavery in their Egyptian bondage (Exod 1:10–14; 5:6–14), from which they eventually were led to be a free people under Moses (Exod 12:37–42). Because of that experience, Mosaic legislation developed certain rules about the keeping of slaves: "Remember that once you were slaves in Egypt and the Lord your God redeemed you; that is why I give you this order today" (Deut 15:15; cf. Lev 25:42–45, 55). Even though slavery as a social and economic institution was recognized in ancient Israel, there was a clear attempt to humanize it in a way that set Israel apart from its neighbors. The social and economic structure of ancient Palestine was not, therefore, built on slavery, as it often was in other contemporary cultures and lands.

The justification of it as an institution was seen in the curse of Canaan uttered by Noah in Gen 9:25–27, in the stipulation about the circumcision of slaves in Gen 17:12–13, 23, 27 and in that set forth in Lev 25:44–46. Note also the directive given by the angel of the Lord to Hagar in Gen 16:9.

(45) In a reflection on his past life Job queried, "If I rejected the cause of my slave or my slave woman when they brought a complaint against me, what then should I do when God rises up? When he makes inquiry, what should I answer? Did not He who made me in the womb make him? And did not the same One fashion us in the womb?" (31:13–15). Exod 21:20 decrees punishment for the Hebrew who fatally strikes his slave, male or female, and Exod 21:26–27 insists on the emancipation of the slave, male or female, whose eye or tooth is knocked out by the master. Moreover the Hebrews were instructed, "Pay no attention to all that people say, lest you hear your slave cursing you; for you know in your heart that you have often cursed others" (Qoh 7:21–22). Hence Hebrew slaves were to be treated within the family household:

> If you acquire a Hebrew slave, he shall serve six years; in the seventh year he shall go forth free, without cost. If he comes to you single, he shall go forth single; if he comes to you as the husband of a wife, his wife shall go forth with him. If his master gives him a wife and she bears him sons or daughters, the woman and her children shall belong to the master, and he shall go forth alone. If, however, the slave declares, "I love my master, my wife, and my children; I will not go forth free," his master shall bring him to God and bring him to the door or the doorpost; his master shall pierce his

> ear with an awl, and he shall serve him forever. If a man sells his daughter as a maidservant, she shall not go free as male slaves do. If she becomes displeasing in the eyes of her master who has designated her for himself, he shall let her be bought free; he has no right to sell her to a foreign people and deal treacherously with her. If he designates her for his son, he shall deal with her as with daughters. (Exod 21:2–9; cf. also Deut 15:12–14, 16–18; Jer 34:8–17)

(46) Similarly, the poor in Israel, who became slaves or indentured servants, were to be liberated in the year of jubilee (Lev 25:39–41). There were also regulations for the treatment of foreign slaves or slaves of resident aliens (Lev 25:44–46a): "You may make slaves of them, but over your brethren the people of Israel you shall not rule, one over another, with harshness" (Lev 25:46b). See Lev 25:47–54 for regulations governing the redeeming or ransom of slaves; and Sir 33:24–31 on the treatment of slaves, especially Sir 33:30–31: "If you have a slave, let him be as yourself, because you have bought him with blood. If you have a slave, treat him as a brother, for as your own soul you will need him. If you mistreat him and he leaves and runs away, which way will you go to look for him?"

(47) It is interesting to note, moreover, how Josephus has interpreted some of these verses:

> Someone sold to one of the same race [i.e. a Hebrew] shall serve him for six years, and in the seventh year he shall be allowed to go free. If, however, children have been born to him from a slave woman of the house of the master who has bought him and he, out of good will and affection for his own, desires to continue to serve him, at the coming of the year of jubilee, i.e. the fiftieth year, he shall be allowed to go free, he and his children and his wife, also free. (*Ant.* 4.8.28 §273)

Josephus has here joined two of the foregoing regulations. He also regards the law made by Herod the Great to punish housebreakers by selling them into slavery to foreigners as "a violation of the laws of the country," because Jews were "not to be sold to foreigners" or "suffer lifelong slavery." They were to be released after six years (*Ant.* 16.1.1 §1–3).

(48) A passage in the Mosaic law that might seem pertinent to the interpretation of the Letter to Philemon is Deut 23:16–17 (15–16E), which reads: "You shall not give up to his master a slave who has escaped from his master to you; he shall dwell with you, in your midst, in the place which you shall choose within one of your towns, where it pleases him best; you shall not oppress him." (See Philo's interpretation of this passage in light of contemporary Greek laws [*De virtutibus* 24 §124; cf. Goodenough, *HTR* 22 (1929) 182].

For the ways in which Deut 23:16–17 was understood in the later rabbinic tradition, see Str-B, 3. 668–70).

That OT passage (Deut 23:16–17), however, does not color Paul's thinking, because Onesimus was not Jewish, but a Gentile, a pagan who was eventually converted to Christianity. Hence Paul's thinking in this letter rather reflects only his Greco-Roman background, scarcely that of the OT.

(49) In postbiblical times of pre-Christian Palestinian Judaism, Josephus tells of Essene Jews who "did not practice the acquiring of slaves," believing that such a practice leads to injustice (*Ant.* 18.1.5 §21). Similarly, Philo reports about the related Therapeutae in Egypt and the Essenes in Palestine, that they have no slaves because the owning of them leads to injustice and is "against nature" (*De vita contemplativa* 9 §70–71; cf. *Quod omnis probus liber* 12 §79; *Hypothetica* 11.4).

Among the Dead Sea Scrolls, however, the Damascus Document, an Essene rule book, speaks of slaves among the members of the community: "Let no one contend(?) with his slave, his slave woman, or his hireling on the Sabbath" (CD 11:12). And again, "Let him not sell his slave or his slave woman to them [i.e. Gentiles], because they came with him into the covenant of Abraham" (CD 12:10–11). Such regulations clearly differ from the testimony of both Josephus and Philo about the Essenes.

See *De specialibus legibus* (2.19 §90–91) for Philo's thoughts on the way slaves were to be treated.

(50) Slavery in Pauline Thinking

Whereas Aristotle denied that there could be *philia* (friendship) with a slave *qua* slave, he admitted that there could be such with a slave considered as *anthrōpos*, "human being" (*Nic. Ethics* 8.13 §1161b). Paul's outlook was considerably different, especially when it came to Christian slaves, for he states in Gal 3:26–28, "As many of you as were baptized into Christ have put on Christ. There is neither Jew nor Greek, neither slave nor free, neither male nor female; for you are all one in Christ Jesus." This unity of Christians in Christ Jesus is an effect of faith and baptism and results in Christian equality. That equality "in Christ Jesus" does not cancel out all cultural, political, or social distinctions. It is rather a unity that transcends the distinctions such as they are. This is made clear by 1 Cor 12:13–14, where Paul says, "Just as a body is one, though it has many members, and all the members of the body, though many, are one body, so too is Christ. For in one Spirit we were all baptized into one body, whether Jews or Greeks, whether slaves or free, and we all were made to drink of one Spirit."

(51) Paul's most explicit treatment of the status of slavery is found in 1 Cor 7:20–24:

> Everyone should remain in the state in which he was called. Were you a slave when you were called? Do not worry about it! But if you can become free, make the most of it. For the slave called in the Lord is a freedman of the Lord; similarly the one who was free when called is a slave of Christ. You have been bought at a price; do not become slaves to human beings. So, brothers, everyone should continue before God in the state in which he was called.

The basis on which this Pauline judgment is made is expressed in 2 Cor 5:17: "Whoever is in Christ is a new creation; things of old have passed away, new things have come to be." This expresses the christological foundation of the way that Paul regards the new Christian status. See further S. S. Bartchy, *Mallon chrēsai,* and the bibliography given on pp. 185–99.

In the Letter to Philemon, Paul formulates the matter a bit differently, for the slave was to be considered not only as *anthrōpos* but as *adelphos,* "brother," i.e. a fellow Christian: "as more than a slave, as a beloved brother. He is such to me, but how much more to you, both as a man and in the Lord" (v 16). To deprive Paul of Onesimus would be to deprive him of his own heart (v 12).

What strikes the modern reader of such Pauline passages is his failure to speak out against the social institution of slavery in general and the injustices that it often involved, not only for the individual so entrapped but also for his wife and children. If I am right in interpreting the "more than I ask" of v 21 as an implicit request made of Philemon to see to the emancipation of Onesimus, that may tell us something about Paul's attitude toward the enslavement of a Christian; but that "more" has been diversely interpreted over the centuries and its sense is not clear. Moreover that is an implicit request about an individual case of a Christian slave who could help Paul in his work of evangelization. Would Paul have written the same thing to the non-Christian owner of a pagan slave? Would he have agreed with Aristotle's view about "friendship" with such a slave?

(52) Slavery in Later Christianity

The basic attitude of Paul toward Christian slavery is continued later on. In Col 3:11 one reads, "Here there is neither Greek nor Jew, circumcised or uncircumcised, barbarian, Scythian, slave, or free, but Christ is all and in all." Rules for Christian slaves, however, are set forth in the *Haustafeln* (domestic or family bulletin boards) of Col 3:22–4:1; Eph 6:5–9; 1 Pet 2:18–21. Compare 1 Tim 6:1–2; Titus 2:9–10.

In the patristic period, the postapostolic writing of the Shepherd of Hermas gives counsel about ransoming slaves in *Mand.* 8.10; *Sim.* 1.8; and advice concerning the handling of slaves is supplied by Ignatius of Antioch, *Polycarp* 4.3. Clement of Rome tells of many who delivered themselves to bondage to ransom others or who gave themselves into slavery to provide food for others (*1 Clem.* 55.2). Still later, John Chrysostom discusses the treatment of slaves in *Hom. 40 in Ep. 1 ad Cor.* (PG 61. 353–545). Details about how writers of the patristic period understood Paul's Letter to Philemon can be found in Mitchell, "John Chrysostom on Philemon."

(53) M. R. Vincent (*Word Studies*, 3. 525–26) once wrote:

> Under Constantine the effects of christian sentiment began to appear in the Church and in legislation concerning slaves. Official freeing of slaves became common as an act of pious gratitude, and burial tablets often represent masters standing before the Good Shepherd, with a band of slaves liberated at death, and pleading for them at judgment. In A.D. 312 a law was passed declaring as homicide the poisoning or branding of slaves, and giving them to be torn by beasts. The advance of a healthier sentiment may be seen by comparing the law of Augustus, which forbade a master to emancipate more than one-fifth of his slaves, and which fixed one hundred males as a maximum for one time—and the unlimited permission to emancipate conceded by Constantine. Each new ruler enacted some measure which facilitated emancipation. Every obstacle was thrown up by law in the way of separating families. Under Justinian all presumptions were in favor of liberty.

IV. Significance of the Letter

◆

(54) Ancient commentators wondered why an ostensibly personal letter with little corporate pastoral concern should have found its way into the Christian canon of Scripture. We have already noted how Onesimus may have been involved in the collection of Paul's letters, which may account partly for the canonical status the letter was eventually accorded. Jerome mentioned people of his day who claimed that the letter *nihil habere quod aedificare nos potest* (has nothing that can edify us, *In Ep. ad Philemonem,* Prologue [PL 26. 637]). For the Letter to Philemon contains none of the usual Pauline teaching. Indeed, there is nothing even about the repentance of Onesimus.

And yet John Chrysostom could say about the letter:

> It is worth learning that this letter was sent about necessary matters. See, then, how many things are set right by it. The first thing is that one should be earnest in all matters. For if Paul displays so much concern about a runaway, a thief, and a robber and does not refuse to send him back with such commendations, and feels no shame about it, how much more does it befit us not to be careless in such matters! Secondly, we should not give up as hopeless the class of slaves, even if they have gone to evil extremes. For if a thief or a runaway became so virtuous that Paul was willing to take him as a partner and wrote about him "that he might serve me on your behalf" [v 13], how much more should we not give up the free as hopeless. (*In Ep. ad Philemonem,* Arg. [PG 62. 705])

(55) The letter, moreover, does have a pastoral concern, for it is addressed to others than Philemon himself, and even to the church that meets in his house. If Paul does not invoke his apostolic authority to demand obedience of Philemon (v 8), he does confront him with a plea for love (vv 8–11, 21). So despite the impression that the letter first makes as one dealing with a personal matter, it embodies an attitude toward slavery that merits widespread attention in the Christian church. It manifests Paul's personal, pastoral, and warm-hearted affection for the slave Onesimus. In sending him back to Philemon, Paul not only recognizes Philemon's legal right but also delicately pleads that Onesimus be treated like a "brother." This is meant not just in the sense of Sir 33:32 ("If you have a servant, treat him as a brother") but also as a "fellow Christian," since this is the connotation of the term *adelphos* in Paul's writings

(see NOTE on "brother" in v 1). Because of this teaching, the Letter to Philemon is not a "strictly private letter," as Lightfoot once maintained (*Colossians and Philemon,* 301) and others have often repeated. It must be regarded rather as "an apostolic writing," even though it concerns an individual (see U. Wickert, ZNW 52 [1961] 230–38; P. Stuhlmacher, *Brief an Philemon,* 17). For the Letter to Philemon proclaims "the early Christian conviction that faith and love should determine the action of the Christian. Whatever the situation in which decision and action are called for, it is to be seen in the context of this Christian foundation for behaviour" (Marshall, "The Theology of Philemon," 187). Moreover the fact that Paul calls attention in v 19 to his writing in his own hand reveals that the letter was envisaged as something to be read to the church that gathered at Philemon's house.

(56) Did Paul mean that Philemon should set the slave Onesimus free? This may be implied, but it is not clearly stated. As a result, the Letter to Philemon has been understood in two basic ways in the course of its historical interpretation:

(a) In the sense that Paul reckons with the social condition of slavery and tries only to interiorize it, i.e. give it a Christian meaning. Nowhere in any of his letters does Paul try to change the existing social structure, which reckoned with slavery, perhaps because he realized the futility of attempting to change the system, which was so much part of the world in which he lived. Paul's own solution would be, then, to emphasize religious renewal and transform, interiorize, or christianize that social structure; recall 1 Cor 7:20–24; 12:13; Rom 13:1–7. Hence in this letter Paul is urging Philemon to welcome Onesimus back as a "beloved brother," because he is a "freedman of the Lord" (1 Cor 7:22), and especially in view of what Paul teaches in Gal 3:27–28, "For as many of you as were baptized into Christ have put on Christ. There is neither Jew nor Greek, neither slave nor free, neither male nor female; for you are all one in Christ Jesus." Moreover his plea in this letter is made "out of love" (v 8). This is the understanding of the Letter to Philemon that was advocated by John Chrysostom (PG 62. 701–4); Theodore of Mopsuestia; Jerome (PL 26. 650); Martin Luther (Deutsche Bibel 7.292; WAusg 25.69; 40/2.3); Hugo Grotius, *Annotationes,* 1642; and among modern interpreters by Bieder, Binder, Dunn, Ewald, Francke, Friedrich, Haupt, Kümmel, Lohse, Lueken, Meyer, Preiss, Schlatter, Suhl, Vincent.

(57) (b) The Letter to Philemon has also been understood in the sense that Paul is mildly criticizing the social structure of slavery and strongly implying the emancipation of Onesimus. Those who have followed this view of the significance of the letter argue from Paul's rhetoric and the thrust of his argument that slavery is ultimately incompatible with Christian teaching and practice. Verse 21 is above all important in this view of the letter, with its plea that Philemon do "even more than I ask." This understanding of it was advocated

by Jean Calvin, Bengel, and among modern interpreters by Lightfoot (*Colossians and Philemon,* 326–27), Marshall, Stuhlmacher. See also H. Koester, *Introduction,* 2. 135; and especially the "Auslegungs- und Wirkungsgeschichte" of the letter written by Stuhlmacher (*Brief an Philemon,* 58–66).

(58) Modern Christians are repulsed by the idea of slavery and often wonder why Paul did not speak out more against such a problem of social justice. Indeed, it took centuries even for what Paul may be implying in this letter to have any effect, especially in the Christian church of the West. The Letter to Philemon provides a Pauline insight into both the social relations of ancient Greco-Roman culture and the relations between masters and slaves, an insight that is surpassed only by what Paul says about the matter in 1 Corinthians. No matter what one wants to say about the role of the Christian church in the problem of slavery over the centuries—and it is a sad story—the Letter to Philemon instills an attitude that must govern even Christians of the twentieth and twenty-first centuries, for as Martin Luther once put it,

> This letter gives us a masterful and tender example of Christian love. For we see here how St. Paul takes the part of poor Onesimus and, as best he can, pleads his cause with his master. He presents himself not otherwise than if he were himself Onesimus, who has done wrong; yet he does this not with force or compulsion, as he had a right to do, but he empties himself of his right to get Philemon too to waive his right. Just as Christ did for us with God the Father, so St. Paul does for Onesimus with Philemon. For Christ emptied himself of his right and overcame the Father with love and humility, so that the Father had to put away his anger and rights and bring us into favor for the sake of Christ, who so earnestly pleads our cause and so heartily takes our part. For we are all his Onesimi, just as we believe. ("Prologue to the Letter of Saint Paul to Philemon," *D. Martin Luthers Werke, Kritische Gesamtausgabe: Die Deutsche Bibel* 7 [Weimar: Böhlaus Nachfolger, 1931] 292–93; cf. *LW,* 35. 390.)

(59) The Letter to Philemon has at times also been considered as an illustration of the principle of the renunciation of rights that Paul advocates in 1 Corinthians 6, where he criticizes Christians who hale other Christians into secular courts and before civil judges to adjudicate differences that arise among them (1:8). See Rapske, "The Prisoner Paul," 196; Lampe, "Keine 'Sklavenflucht,' " 137.

V. Theological Teaching of the Letter

◆

(60) Petersen maintains that "theology is a form of systematic reflection upon prior knowledge" or upon "a symbolic universe" or its parts (*Rediscovering Paul,* 202), and in this sense "the Letter to Philemon is not 'theological' " (ibid., 201). That is why he is interested rather in its sociology. However, I am using the word "theological" in its more traditional sense of a systematic reflection on the faith that is expressed in the Letter to Philemon.

(61) One will look in vain in the Letter to Philemon for most of the usual topics of Pauline theology. In other letters Paul strives to present the effects of the Christ-event, ten of which can be counted (see *PAHT,* 59–71 §67–80). Here, however, there is none of that. There is no mention of human sin *(hamartia)* or any pardon of it. Nothing is said even of Onesimus' repentance or regret, or of any forgiveness of a wrong that he may have done to his master Philemon. Nothing in the letter recalls the prime Pauline teaching about justification by grace through faith, and not by deeds of the law. Indeed, "grace" *(charis),* though it appears in the initial greeting and concluding salutation (vv 3, 25), is only a part of set formulas, with no developed teaching about it.

Furthermore there is no mention of baptism, not even when Paul speaks of Onesimus as "my child . . . whose father I have become in my imprisonment" (v 10). We never hear how Onesimus became a believing Christian. Although Paul has given some treatment to slavery in other letters (see §50–51 above), there is little discussion of that topic in this letter. The result is that, theologically considered, the Letter to Philemon is not a primary example of Pauline teaching. One can understand, then, why some of the ancients complained about its having "nothing to edify us" (see §54 above). Part of the problem is the type of letter that Paul writes in this instance. It is an *ad hoc* petitionary letter about a particular slave who has become a Christian. The letter, however, has a number of points, some even like *obiter dicta,* which would have to be incorporated into any comprehensive treatment of Pauline theology.

(62) "God" is mentioned twice in the letter, and then only in formulaic expressions, as Paul sends greetings of grace and peace from "God our Father and the Lord Jesus Christ" (v 3) or as he thanks "my God" for the good reports that he has heard about Philemon's faith and love (v 4). There is no discussion

about God, apart from that mention of the Father of all Christians. However, God's provident concern is implied in v 15, where Paul asserts that Onesimus has been separated from Philemon for a while. The verb *echōristhē*, "has been separated," is undoubtedly to be understood as a theological passive, denoting a providential separation of Onesimus from Philemon *by God* (see NOTE on v 15). That hints at a heavenly determination that the coming relationship of Philemon and Onesimus has to be considered on a level higher than that merely of master and slave. To speak of God as "Father" is to speak symbolically, as Petersen rightly states (*Rediscovering Paul*, 27), but that cannot be understood simply by explaining that God is an actor in Paul's story. For Paul, God does act on the social universe of human beings. As Soards rightly stresses, "It is hard to imagine that God who gives and receives in this way [through Philemon's faith and love] was a mere social fact present only in a symbolic universe, but in fact, otherwise absent from the social universe" ("Some Neglected Theological Dimensions," 215), as Petersen seems to maintain (ibid., 27–28). There is more to Pauline teaching in the Letter to Philemon than "the sociology of narrative actions" (*Rediscovering Paul*, 29).

(63) Moreover the Holy Spirit is never mentioned in the letter, and nothing appears about the Spirit's role in Christian life or in that of the specific Christians who are mentioned. Apart from the formulas in the initial greeting (v 3) and the concluding salutation (v 25), *Kyrios*, the symbolic title of the risen Christ used so frequently in other Pauline letters, appears only in vv 5, 16, 20; and in the last two instances in the formulaic prepositional phrase *en Kyriō*, "in the Lord," where the nuance is that of "as a Christian." Only in v 5 of the thanksgiving does *Kyrios Iēsous* express the object of Philemon's faith. *Kyrios* means "master," but it is never used in this common sense to denote the owner of Onesimus, i.e. Philemon, and its absence in this sense is itself significant, because it enhances the symbolic sense in which the risen Christ is the Lord of all, of Paul, of Philemon, of Onesimus, and of all the others mentioned by name in the letter.

(64) "Christ" is mentioned in vv 1, 3, 6, 8, 9, 20, 23, 25, and once again only in formulaic phrases in most instances, but in v 6 there is undoubtedly a teleological connotation, when Paul speaks of "all the good that is ours" unto Christ *(eis Christon)*, a phrase with diverse interpretations (see NOTE on v 6). There is no development of christological teaching in the letter.

(65) "The church at your house" is among the addressees of the letter (v 2), and it is seen to be involved intimately in the plea that Paul makes for Onesimus, but it does not become a topic of ecclesiological discussion. Nor is it described otherwise as the collective entity of Christians, even though Philemon, Apphia, Archippus, and the members of that house congregation must be understood as aware of their group relationship and considered to be concerned about Onesimus. To them the individuals who send greetings in

vv 23–24 are clearly known and perhaps in some way related to that house-church.

(66) Paul writes this letter from prison, and is "a prisoner . . . for Christ Jesus" (vv 1, 9). Even if he is silent about where he is imprisoned or about details of his arrest, he ascribes that imprisonment to "the gospel" (v 13), i.e. to the good news of Jesus Christ, which has its origin in God (1 Thess 2:2; Rom 1:1) and which proclaims Jesus Christ as Lord (2 Cor 4:4–5); see further *PAHT*, 38–41 §31–36. In this letter Paul does not develop further an aspect of "the gospel," but notes only that he is imprisoned because of it and desires to have Onesimus back so that he may assist Paul in Philemon's stead in the service of the gospel (v 13). Thus Paul's plea to Philemon is rooted in his concern for the good news that he preaches about "Christ crucified" (1 Cor 1:23).

(67) In other letters Paul describes the human reaction or response to the gospel (the preached Word) as "faith" (*pistis*, esp. Rom 10:8–10; cf. *PAHT*, 84–86 §109–11). In this letter he recalls that he has heard about Philemon's faith in the Lord Jesus (v 5). He means thereby not just that he learned that Philemon believes in the risen Christ but recognizes how his vital faith has been operative in "love for all God's dedicated people." He further prays that the sharing in the faith of Philemon by God's dedicated people may promote the realization of all the good that comes to Christians unto Christ (*eis Christon*, v 6). So Paul makes much of Philemon's faith reaction to the "gospel."

(68) Related to Philemon's faith is his love (*agapē*, vv 5, 7), for Paul sees Philemon as an example of "faith working itself out through love," about which he once wrote in Gal 5:6. This love is Philemon's outgoing concern for all God's dedicated people (*eis pantas tous hagious*, v 5), and it is directed also toward Paul himself (v 7). Because Philemon is known for such love, Paul makes his plea with him *dia tēn agapēn*, "out of love," rather than pressing his apostolic authority on him (v 9). Also for this reason Paul addresses Philemon as "beloved" (*agapētos*, v 1). Strikingly, he uses the identical adjective of Onesimus, the newborn Christian in v 16. So for Paul, not only is Philemon "beloved" but also the slave Onesimus. Because of this relationship, Paul can plead with Philemon to welcome the slave as he would welcome the Apostle himself (v 17).

(69) This emphasis on love in the Letter to Philemon leads to Paul's teaching about brotherhood. Paul not only calls Timothy, the cosender of the letter, a "brother" (*adelphos*, v 1) and addresses it to Apphia as a "sister" *(adelphē)* but twice addresses Philemon himself as *adelphe*, "brother" (vv 7, 20), because *adelphos* and *adelphē* have become for Paul symbolic titles that express one's Christian status. Hence the main plea in his letter is that Philemon welcome Onesimus back as more than a slave, as a "beloved brother" (v 16), as he is

especially to Paul. In other words, the mutual relationship of love and brotherhood that already exists between Paul and Philemon must now be widened consciously and accorded even to the slave Onesimus. Philemon and Onesimus are no longer to be thought of as master and slave, but as brothers, and that on a double level, *kai en sarki kai en Kyriō*, "as a human being" and "in the Lord" (v 16c), i.e. as Christians. This indirectly tells us a little about how Paul conceived the social relations among members of the Christian church. They are expected to react as human beings, but also as Christians.

(70) At one point Paul notes that Onesimus "perhaps has been separated for a while" from Philemon so that he might "have him back for good" (v 15). Underlying this view of the relationship of Philemon and Onesimus is the Pauline understanding of all Christian life: "There is neither Jew nor Greek, neither slave nor free, neither male nor female, for you are all one in Christ Jesus" (Gal 3:28). For Onesimus is now "in the Lord" (v 16c), and as such he is "more than a slave" (v 16a). Onesimus may have to retain the social status that he always had, but a Christian master should no longer regard him, who is now also a Christian, only from that human and social point of view. As in other letters, Paul uses the prepositional phrase "in the Lord" as a way of expressing the intimate relation of a believing Christian to the risen Christ. It has often been understood in a local, spatial sense connoting the spiritual atmosphere in which Christians are bathed "in Christ" (often identified with his Spirit). With *Kyrios* the preposition *en* denotes the dynamic influence that the risen Lord has on the practical and ethical areas of Christian conduct; that is the sense in which it is employed here in the Letter to Philemon; see further *PAHT*, 89–90 §121.

(71) Finally, Paul recalls to Philemon "all the good that is ours in Christ" (v 6), or "unto Christ." This is the one verse in the letter in which Paul may be thinking teleologically, because the prepositional phrase *eis Christon*, with which the verse ends, seems to express the goal of Christian conduct: the good that comes to Christians through faith working itself out in love has a destination or *finis* toward which it is ultimately determined, perhaps for the glory of Christ (see NOTE on v 6).

VI. STRUCTURE AND OUTLINE OF THE LETTER

◆

(72) OUTLINE

The structure of the Letter to Philemon can be seen thus:

(I) Introduction: Prescript and greeting (1–3)
(II) Thanksgiving: Thanks to God for Philemon's faith and love (4–7)
(III) Body: Appeal to Philemon's goodwill to welcome back Onesimus and a hint at his usefulness to Paul (8–20)
(IV) Conclusion: Final instruction, greetings, and blessing (21–25)

This outline is also used by Collange, *L'Epître*, 24; Dunn, *Colossians and Philemon*, 309; Lohse, *Colossians and Philemon;* R. P. Martin, *Ephesians*, 141–42; Stuhlmacher, *Brief an Philemon*, 24; Vincent, *Philippians and Philemon*.

Some commentators, however, prefer to make the body of the letter only vv 8–16. Then vv 17–22 form its epilogue or peroration; the conclusion comes in vv 23–25. So Bartchy, *ABD*, 5. 305; Gnilka, *Philemonbrief*, 7–9; Patzia, "Philemon, Letter to," 704. For Carson (*Colossians and Philemon*), the conclusion begins at v 22.

(73) Some interpreters consider the thanksgiving to be limited to vv 4–6 (so Lohmeyer, *Kolosser und Philemon*, 179; Schubert, *Form and Function*, 44, 65; O'Brien, *Introductory Thanksgivings*, 48–49); for them the body would begin with v 7, but the majority of interpreters make v 7 part of the thanksgiving, as I have done, because of its thought content, even though it is added to the basic four elements of a thanksgiving that Schubert has noted. Moreover the body clearly begins in v 8, being introduced by the particle *dio*, "so, accordingly."

(74) Those who emphasize the rhetorical aspect of the Letter to Philemon note that after the epistolary prescript, elements of deliberative rhetoric can be found in it: Paul's exordium in vv 4–7; the body or rhetorical proof in vv 8–16; and the peroration in vv 17–20 (see Quintilian, *Inst.* 3.8.1–15; 6.2.9–14;

Aristotle, *Rhetoric* 3.14–19). Despite such rhetorical elements in the writing, it is still a letter (with prescript and conclusion), and specifically a letter of petition. See further F. F. Church, "Rhetorical Structure"; P.-L. Couchoud, "Le style rhythmé"; S. B. C. Winter, "Methodological Observations"; and Schenk, *ANRW* 3446–70 (where the rhetorical analysis of the letter's twenty-five verses is greatly overdone).

(75) In its structure, this letter follows the normal shape of a Pauline letter (see Fitzmyer, "Introduction to New Testament Epistles," *NJBC*, art. 45, §8; cf. Lohse, *Colossians and Philemon*, 187).

VII. Bibliography for the Introduction

◆

(76) *General*

Baur, F. C., *Paulus, der Apostel Jesu Christi: Sein Leben und Wirken, seine Briefe und seine Lehre* (2 vols.; 2d ed., rev. E. Zeller; Leipzig: Fue's Verlag, 1866–67), 2. 88–94; *Paul, the Apostle of Jesus Christ: His Life and Work, His Epistles and His Doctrine* (London: Williams & Norgate, 1875–76), 2. 80–84.

Benoit, P., "Philémon (Epître à)," *DBSup*, 7. 1204–11.

Bruce, F. F., "St. Paul in Rome: 2. The Epistle to Philemon," *BJRL* 48 (1965–66) 81–97.

Cadoux, C. J., "The Date and Provenance of the Imprisonment Epistles of St. Paul," *ExpTim* 45 (1933–34) 471–73.

Callahan, A. D., "John Chrysostom on Philemon: A Response to Margaret M. Mitchell," *HTR* 88 (1995) 149–56.

———, "Paul's Epistle to Philemon: Toward an Alternative *Argumentum*," *HTR* 86 (1993) 357–76.

Church, F. F., "Rhetorical Structure and Design in Paul's Letter to Philemon," *HTR* 71 (1978) 17–33.

Cope, L., "On Rethinking the Philemon-Colossians Connection," *BR* 30 (1985) 45–50.

Couchoud, P.-L., "Le style rhythmé dans l'épître de Saint Paul à Philémon," *RHR* 96 (1927) 129–46; 97 (1928) 189–91.

Dahl, N. A., "The Particularity of the Pauline Epistles as a Problem in the Ancient Church," *Neotestamentica et patristica: Eine Freundesgabe, Herrn Professor Dr. Oscar Cullmann . . .* (NovTSup 6; ed. W. C. van Unnik; Leiden: Brill, 1962) 260–71, esp. 264–65.

Dearing, V. A., *A Manual of Textual Analysis* (Berkeley and Los Angeles: University of California, 1959; repr. Westport, Conn.: Greenwood, 1983) 86–93.

Duncan, G. S., "Important Hypothesis Reconsidered: VI. Were Paul's Imprisonment Epistles Written from Ephesus?" *ExpTim* 67 (1955–56) 163–66.

———, *St Paul's Ephesian Ministry: A Reconstruction with Special Reference to the Ephesian Origin of the Imprisonment Epistles* (London: Hodder and Stoughton, 1929; New York: Scribner's Sons, 1930) 72–75.

Glaze, R. E., "Onesimus: Runaway or Emissary?" *Theological Educator* 54 (1996) 3–11.

Goodenough, E. R., "Paul and Onesimus," *HTR* 22 (1929) 181–83.

Greeven, H., "Prüfung der Thesen von J. Knox zum Philemonbrief," *TLZ* 79 (1954) 373–78.

Harrill, J. A., Review of A. D. Callahan, *Embassy of Onesimus: The Letter to Philemon, CBQ* 60 (1998) 757–59.

Harrison, P. N., "Onesimus and Philemon," *ATR* 32 (1950) 268–94.

Holtzmann, H. J., "Der Brief an den Philemon, kritisch untersucht," *ZWT* 16 (1873) 428–41.

Kirkland, A., "The Beginnings of Christianity in the Lycus Valley: An Exercise in Historical Reconstruction," *Neotestamentica* 29 (1995) 109–24.

Knox, J., *Philemon among the Letters of Paul: A New View of Its Place and Importance* (Chicago: University of Chicago, 1935); *Revised Edition* (Nashville, Tenn., and New York: Abingdon; London: Collins, 1959).

———, "Philemon and the Authenticity of Colossians," *JR* 18 (1938) 144–60.

Lampe, P., "Keine 'Sklavenflucht' des Onesimus," *ZNW* 76 (1985) 135–37.

Manen, W. C. van, "Philemon, Epistle to," *Encyclopaedia biblica* (4 vols.; New York: Macmillan, 1899–1903), 3. 3693–97.

Marshall, I. H., "The Theology of Philemon," in *The Theology of the Shorter Pauline Letters* (New Testament Theology; ed. K. P. Donfried and I. H. Marshall; Cambridge: Cambridge University, 1993) 175–91.

Martens, J. W., "Ignatius and Onesimus: John Knox Reconsidered," *Second Century* 9 (1992) 73–86.

Metzger, B. M., *The Text of the New Testament: Its Transmission, Corruption, and Restoration* (3d ed.; New York and Oxford: Oxford University Press, 1992).

Mitchell, M. M., "John Chrysostom on Philemon: A Second Look," *HTR* 88 (1995) 135–48.

Mitton, C. L., *The Formation of the Pauline Corpus of Letters* (London: Epworth, 1955) 50–54.

Mommsen, T., et al. (eds.), *The Digest of Justinian* (4 vols.; Philadelphia, Pa.: University of Pennsylvania, 1985).

Nordling, J. G., "Onesimus Fugitivus: A Defense of the Runaway Slave Hypothesis in Philemon," *JSNT* 41 (1991) 97–119.

Petersen, N. R., *Rediscovering Paul: Philemon and the Sociology of Paul's Narrative World* (Philadelphia, Pa.: Fortress, 1985).

Preuschen, E., *Analecta: Kürzere Texte zur Geschichte der Alten Kirche und des Kanons II* (2d ed.; Tübingen: Mohr [Siebeck], 1910) 87.

Rapske, B. M., "The Prisoner Paul in the Eyes of Onesimus," *NTS* 37 (1991) 187–203.

Reicke, B., "Caesarea, Rome, and the Captivity Epistles," *Apostolic History and the Gospel: Biblical and Historical Essays Presented to F. F. Bruce . . .* (ed. W. W. Gasque and R. P. Martin; Grand Rapids, Mich.: Eerdmans, 1970) 277–86.

Roberts, J. H., "Teologie en etiek in die brief aan Filemon: 'n Poging tot verantwoording," *Skrif en Kerk* 14/1 (1993) 105–15.

Robinson, J. A. T., *Redating the New Testament* (London: SCM; Philadelphia, Pa.: Westminster, 1976), 61–67.

Schenk, W., "Der Brief des Paulus an Philemon in der neueren Forschung (1945–1987)," *ANRW* 2/25.4 (1987) 3439–95.

Schulz, D., "Sollte der Apostel Paulus wirklich nicht in Colossä und Laodicea gewesen seyn?" *TSK* 2 (1829) 535–38.

Soards, M. L., "Some Neglected Theological Dimensions of Paul's Letter to Philemon," *PRS* 17 (1990) 209–19.

Steck, R., "Plinius im Neuen Testament," *Jahrbücher für protestantische Theologie* 17 (1891) 545–84.

Suhl, A., *Paulus und seine Briefe: Ein Beitrag zur paulinischen Chronologie* (SNT 11; Gütersloh: Mohn, 1975).

Weizsäcker, C., *Das apostolische Zeitalter der christlichen Kirche* (Freiburg im B.: Mohr, 1886).

White, J. L., "The Structural Analysis of Philemon: A Point of Departure in the Formal Analysis of the Pauline Letter," SBLSP 1971 (Missoula, Mont.: Society of Biblical Literature, 1971) 1–47.

Wickert, U., "Der Philemonbrief—Privatbrief oder apostolisches Schreiben?" *ZNW* 52 (1961) 230–38.

Winter, S. B. C., "Methodological Observations on a New Interpretation of Paul's Letter to Philemon," *USQR* 39 (1984) 203–12.

———, "Paul's Letter to Philemon," *NTS* 33 (1987) 1–15.

Zmijewski, J., "Beobachtungen zur Struktur des Philemonbriefes," *BibLeb* 15 (1974) 273–96; repr. *Das Neue Testament: Quelle christlicher Theologie und Glaubenspraxis* (Stuttgart: Katholisches Bibelwerk, 1986) 129–55.

(77) *Slavery in Antiquity*

Alföldi, G., "Die Freilassung von Sklaven und die Struktur der Sklaverei in der römischen Kaiserzeit," *Rivista storica dell'antichità* 2 (1972) 97–129.

Allard, P., *Les esclaves chrétiens depuis les premiers temps de l'église jusqu'à la fin de la domination romaine en Occident* (2d ed.; Paris: Didier, 1876).

Arzt, P., "Brauchbare Sklaven: Ausgewählte Papyrustexte zum Philemonbrief," *Protokolle zur Bibel* 1 (1992) 44–58.

Barnes, A., *An Inquiry into the Scriptural Views of Slavery* (Philadelphia, Pa.: Perkins & Purves, 1846; Philadelphia, Pa.: Parry & McMillan, 1855; repr. Detroit, Mich.: Negro History [1969]) 318–31.

Barrow, R. H., *Slavery in the Roman Empire* (London: Methuen; New York: Barnes and Noble, 1928; repr. 1968).

Bartchy, S. S., *Mallon chrēsai: First Century Slavery and the Interpretation of 1 Corinthians 7:21* (SBLDS 11; Missoula, Mont.: Scholars, 1973; repr. Atlanta, Ga.: Scholars, 1985).

Bellen, H., *Studien zur Sklavenflucht im römischen Kaiserreich* (Forschungen zur antiken Sklaverei 4; Wiesbaden: Steiner, 1971) 78–92.

Bojorge, H., "La intercesión por un esclavo: Pablo a Filemón y Plinio a Sabiniano," *RevistB* 42 (1980) 159–69.

Bömer, F., *Untersuchungen über die Religion der Sklaven in Griechenland und Rom, Teil 1–4* (Wiesbaden: Steiner, 1958–63).

Borelli, G., *Schiavitù e liberazione in Paolo e nella dialettica marxista* (Genoa: Lanterna, 1978).

Bourne, G., *A Condensed Anti-Slavery Bible Argument* (New York: Benedict, 1845) 82–84.

Bradley, K. R., *Slavery and Society at Rome* (Cambridge: Cambridge University, 1994).

———, *Slaves and Masters in the Roman Empire: A Study in Social Control* (Collection Latomus 185; Brussels: Latomus, 1984).

Buckland, W. W., *The Roman Law of Slavery: The Condition of the Slave in Private Law from Augustus to Justinian* (Cambridge: Cambridge University, 1908; repr. New York: AMS, 1969).

Coleman-Norton, P. R., "The Apostle Paul and the Roman Law of Slavery," *Studies in Roman Economic and Social History in Honor of Allan Chester Johnson* (ed. P. R. Coleman-Norton; Princeton, N.J.: Princeton University, 1951; repr. Freeport, N.Y.: Books for Libraries, 1969) 155–77.

Corcoran, G., "Slavery in the New Testament," *Milltown Studies* 5 (1980) 1–40.

Eck, W., and J. Heinrichs (eds.), *Sklaven und Freigelassene in der Gesellschaft der römischen Kaiserzeit* (TzF 61; Darmstadt: Wissenschaftliche Buchgesellschaft, 1993).

Fee, J. G., *An Anti-Slavery Manual* (Maysville, Ky.: Herald Office, 1848; repr. New York: Arno, 1969) 112–13.

Finley, M. I. (ed.), *Slavery in Classical Antiquity: Views and Controversies* (2d ed.; Cambridge: Heffer & Sons, 1960).

———, *Ancient Slavery and Modern Ideology* (London: Chatto & Windus; New York: Viking, 1980).

Gayer, R., *Die Stellung des Sklaven in den paulinischen Gemeinden und bei Paulus: Zugleich ein sozialgeschichtlich vergleichender Beitrag zur Wertung *des Sklaven in der Antike* (Europäische Hochschulschriften 23, Theologie 78; Bern and Frankfurt am M.: Lang, 1976) 223–68.

Giles, K., "The Biblical Argument for Slavery: Can the Bible Mislead? A Case Study in Hermeneutics," *EvQ* 66 (1994) 3–17.

Gülzow, H., *Christentum und Sklaverei in den ersten drei Jahrhunderten* (Bonn: Habelt, 1969) 29–41 et passim.

Hopkins, K., and P. J. Roscoe, "Between Slavery and Freedom: On Freeing Slaves at Delphi," *Conquerors and Slaves: Sociological Studies in Roman History, Volume 1* (ed. K. Hopkins; Cambridge: Cambridge University, 1978) 133–71.

Kehnscherper, G., *Die Stellung der Bibel und der alten christlichen Kirche zur Slaverei* (Halle an d. S.: Niemeyer, 1957).

Keppler, P. W. von, "Die Sklavenfrage im Neuen Testament," *TQ* 73 (1891) 218–86.

Laub, F., *Die Begegnung des frühen Christentums mit der antiken Sklaverei* (SBS 107; Stuttgart: Katholisches Bibelwerk, 1982) 63–75.

Lauffer, S., "Die Sklaverei in der griechisch-römischen Welt," *Gymnasium* 68 (1961) 370–95.

Lyall, F., "Roman Law in the Writings of Paul—the Slave and the Freedman," *NTS* 17 (1970–71) 73–79.

Möhler, J. A., *Bruckstücke aus der Geschichte der Aufhebung der Sklaverei* (Gesammelte Schriften und Aufsätze; Regensburg: Manz, 1840), 2. 54–140.

Morrison, L. R., "The Religious Defense of American Slavery before 1830," *Journal of Religious Thought* 37/2 (1980–81) 16–29.

Nordling, J. G., "Christ Leavens Culture: St. Paul on Slavery," *ConcJ* 24 (1998) 43–52, esp. 50.

O'Brien, P. T., *Introductory Thanksgivings in the Letters of Paul* (NovTSup 49; Leiden: Brill, 1977) 47–61.

Osiek, C., "Slavery in the New Testament World," *TBT* 22 (1984) 151–55.

Raffeiner, H., *Sklaven und Freigelassene: Eine soziologische Studie auf der Grundlage des griechischen Grabepigramms* (Philologie und Epigraphik 2; Innsbruck: Wagner, 1977).

Roberti, M., *La lettera di S. Paolo a Filemone e la condizione giuridica dello schiavo fuggitivo* (Pubblicazioni della Università cattolica del Sacro Cuore, ser. II/40; Milan: Società editrice "Vita e Pensiero," 1933).

Rupprecht, A. A., "Attitudes on Slavery among the Church Fathers," *New Dimensions in New Testament Study* (ed. R. N. Longenecker and M. C. Tenney; Grand Rapids, Mich.: Zondervan, 1974) 261–77.

Scheidel, W., "Quantifying the Sources of Slaves in the Early Roman Empire," *JRS* 87 (1997) 156–69.

Schubert, P., *Form and Function of the Pauline Thanksgivings* (BZNW 20: Berlin: Töpelmann, 1939).

Schulz, S., *Gott ist kein Sklavenhalter: Die Geschichte einer verspäteten Revolution* (Zurich: Flamberg; Hamburg: Furche, 1972).

Schulz-Falkenthal, H., *Sklaverei in der griechisch-römischen Antike: Eine Bibliographie wissenschaftlicher Literatur vom ausgehenden 15. Jahrhundert bis zur Mitte des 19. Jahrhunderts* (Halle an d. S.: Universitäts- und Landesbibliothek Sachsen-Anhalt, 1985).

Schweizer, E., "Zum Sklavenproblem im Neuen Testament," *EvT* 32 (1972) 502–6.

Sherwin-White, A. N., *Roman Society and Roman Law in the New Testament* (Sarum Lectures 1960–1961; Oxford: Clarendon, 1963).

Smith, H. S., *In His Image, but . . . Racism in Southern Religion, 1780–1910* (Durham, N.C.: Duke University, 1972).

Sokolowski, F., "The Real Meaning of Sacral Manumission," *HTR* 47 (1954) 173–81.

Söllner, A., *Einführung in die römische Rechtsgeschichte* (2d ed.; Munich: Beck, 1980).

Steinmann, A., *Paulus und die Sklaven zu Korinth: 1. Kor. 7, 21 aufs Neue untersucht* (Braunsberg: H. Grimme, 1911).

———, *Sklavenlos und alte Kirche: Eine historisch-exegetische Studie über die soziale Frage im Urchristentum* (2d ed.; M. Gladbach: Volksverein-V., 1910) 68–72.

Theissen, G., *Wert und Status des Menschen im Urchristentum* (Humanistische Bildung 12; Stuttgart: Württembergischer Verein der Freunde der humanistischen Gymnasiums, 1988) 61–93.

Tourmagne, A. (pseudonym for A. Villard), *Histoire de l'esclavage ancien et moderne* (Paris: Guillaumin & Cie., 1880).

Urbach, E. E., "The Laws Regarding Slavery: As a Source for Social History of the Period of the Second Temple, the Mishnah and Talmud," *Papers of the Institute of Jewish Studies London, Volume 1* (ed. J. G. Weiss; Jerusalem: Magnes, 1964; repr. Lanham, Md.: University Press of America, 1969) 1–94.

Vogt, J., *Ancient Slavery and the Ideal of Man* (Cambridge, Mass.: Harvard University, 1975).

———, *Sklaverei und Humanität: Studien zur antiken Sklaverei und ihrer Erforschung* (Historia-Einzelschriften 8; Wiesbaden: Steiner, 1965; 2d ed., 1972).

Vogt, J., and H. Bellen, *Bibliographie zur antiken Sklaverei* (rev. E. Hermann with N. Brockmeyer; Bochum: Studienverlag Dr. N. Brockmeyer, 1983).

Watson, A., *Roman Slave Law* (Baltimore, Md.: Johns Hopkins University, 1987).

Westermann, W. L., *The Slave Systems of Greek and Roman Antiquity* (Philadelphia, Pa.: American Philosophical Society, 1955; 3d ed., 1964) 90–92, 126–28, 153.

Wiedemann, T. E. J., *Greek and Roman Slavery* (Baltimore, Md.: Johns Hopkins University; London: Croom Helm, 1981) 191–92.

———, "The Regularity of Manumission at Rome," *ClassQ* 35 (1985) 162–75.

Wolff, H. W., "Masters and Slaves: On Overcoming Class-Struggle in the Old Testament," *Int* 27 (1973) 259–72.

Zahn, T., *Sclaverei und Christentum in der alten Welt* (Skizzen aus dem Leben der alten Kirche; Heidelberg: Winter, 1879; repr. Leipzig: Deichert, 1908) 116–59.

General Bibliography

◆

I. Commentaries

A. Patristic Period

1. GREEK WRITERS

Cramer, John A. (1793–1848), *Catenae graecorum patrum in Novum Testamentum* (8 vols.; Oxford: Typographeum Academicum, 1840–44; repr. Hildesheim: Olms, 1967), 7. 103–11.

Staab, K., *Die Pauluskatenen nach den handschriftlichen Quellen untersucht* (SPIB; Rome: Biblical Institute, 1926).

———, *Pauluskommentare aus der griechischen Kirche: Aus Katenenhandschriften gesammelt und herausgegeben* (NTAbh 15; Münster in W.: Aschendorff, 1933).

John Chrysostom (347–407), *In Ep. ad Philemonem Commentarius,* PG 62. 701–20.

See B. Goodall, *The Homilies of St. John Chrysostom on the Letters of St. Paul to Titus and Philemon: Prolegomena to an Edition* (University of California Publications in Classical Studies 20; Berkeley, Calif.: University of California, 1979); "Homilies of St. John Chrysostom . . . on the Epistle of St. Paul the Apostle to Philemon," *A Select Library of the Nicene and Post-Nicene Fathers of the Christian Church* (ed. P. Schaff; New York: Christian Literature Co., 1889), 1/13. 545–57.

Theodore of Mopsuestia (350–428), *In Ep. Pauli ad Philemona commentarii fragmenta,* PG 66. 949–50.

See H. B. Swete, *Theodori episcopi Mopsuesteni in epistolas b. Pauli commentarii: The Latin Version with the Greek Fragments* (2 vols.; Cambridge: Cambridge University, 1880, 1882), 2. 258–85.

Severian of Gabala (fl. ca. 400), in K. Staab, *Pauluskommentare,* 345.

Theodoret of Cyrrhus (393–460), *Interpretatio Ep. ad Philemonem,* PG 82. 871–78.

Oecumenius of Tricca (6th cent. [rightly attributed?]), *Argumentum Ep. ad Philemonem,* PG 119. 261–72; cf. K. Staab, *Pauluskommentare,* 462.

John of Damascus (655–750), *In Ep. ad Philemonem,* PG 95. 1029–34.

2. LATIN WRITERS

Jerome (345–420), *In Ep. ad Philemonem,* PL 26. 635–56.

Ambrosiaster (ca. 366–84), *In Ep. b. Pauli ad Philemonem,* PL 17.531–36; in H. J. Vogels, *Ambrosiaster* (CSEL 81/3) 337–42.

See H. J. Vogels, *Das Corpus Paulinum des Ambrosiaster* (BBB 13; Bonn: Hanstein, 1957) 176–78.

Pelagius (4th–5th cent.), *In Ep. ad Philemonem,* PLSup 1. 1373–74.

John the Deacon (= Pseudo-Jerome) (6th cent.), *In Ep. ad Philemonem,* PL 30. 945–46

Cassiodorus, Flavius M. A. (= Pseudo-Primasius) (487–580), *Ad Philemonem ep. d. Pauli,* PL 68. 683–86.

B. Medieval Period

1. GREEK WRITERS

Photius of Constantinople (810–895), in K. Staab, *Pauluskommentare,* 637.

Theophylact (1050/60–1125?), *In Ep. ad Philemonem,* PG 125. 171–84.

Euthymius Zigabenus (early 12th cent.), *Commentarius in xiv epistulas Sancti Pauli et vii catholicas* (2 vols.; ed. N. Calogeras; Athens: Perri Bros., 1887), 2. 333–40.

2. LATIN WRITERS

Alcuin (740–804), *In Ep. Pauli ad Philemonem,* PL 100. 1025–32.

Claudius of Turin (d. after 827), *Expositio Ep. ad Philemonem,* PL 104. 911–18.

Walafrid Strabo (808–849), *Ep. ad Philemonem,* PL 114. 641–42.

Rabanus Maurus (784–856), *Expositio in Ep. ad Philemonem,* PL 112. 693–712.

Sedulius Scotus (d. ca. 858), *In Ep. ad Philemonem,* PL 103. 249–52.

Haymo of Auxerre (= Pseudo-Haymo of Halberstadt) (d. 865), *In Ep. ad Philemonem,* PL 117. 813–20.

Florus of Lyons (790–860), *In Ep. ad Philemonem,* PL 119. 411–12.

Hatto of Vercelli (924–961), *Expositio in Ep. ad Philemonem,* PL 134. 719–26.

Lanfranc of Bec, Archbishop of Canterbury (1003–89), *Ep. b. Pauli apostoli ad Philemonem,* PL 150. 371–76.

Bruno the Carthusian (1032–1101), *Ep. ad Philemonem,* PL 153. 483–88.

Hervaeus of Châteauroux (1080–1150), *In Ep. ad Philemonem,* PL 181. 1505–20.

Peter Lombard (1100–60), *In Ep. ad Philemonem,* PL 192. 393–98.

Thomas Aquinas (1225–74), *Ep. ad Philemonem,* in *Opera omnia* (25 vols.; Parma: P. Fiaccadori, 1852–73; repr. New York: Musurgia, 1948–50), 13. 661–65.

C. FIFTEENTH- TO EIGHTEENTH-CENTURY WRITERS

Denis the Carthusian (Denys Ryckel) 1402–71), "Enarratio in Epistolam beati Pauli ad Philemonem," *Opera omnia* (Monthou-sur-Bièvre: Typi Cartusiae S. M. de Pratis, 1901), 13. 461–65.

Erasmus, Desiderius (1469–1536), "In Ep. Pauli ad Philemonem argumentum," *Paraphrases in Novum Testamentum* . . . (3 vols.; Berlin: Haude et Spener, 1780), 3. 764–68; cf. *Collected Works of Erasmus* (ed. R. D. Sider; Toronto: University of Toronto, 1993), 44. 69–74; *Opera omnia* (13 vols.; ed. J. Clericus; Leiden, 1705; repr. Hildesheim: Olms, 1962), 6. 977–80.

Luther, Martin (1483–1546), "Auslegung des Philemonbriefes" (1527), *D. Martin Luthers Werke, Kritische Gesamtausgabe* (Weimar: H. Böhlaus Nachfolger, 1902), 25. 69–78; see also the translation of the letter (1522, 1546) and its prologue, *Deutsche Bibel* 7, 292–97; cf. J. Pelikan (tr.), "Lectures on Philemon," *LW*, 29. 91–105.

See G. Buchwald, "Luthers Auslegung des Philemonbriefes," *Allgemeine evangelisch-lutherische Kirchenzeitung* 60 (1927) 391–97.

Bugenhagen, J. (Pomeranus) (1485–1558), *Annotationes in epistolas Pauli ad Gal., etc.* (2d ed.; Nuremberg, 1525; Strassburg, 1534) 135–38.

Calvin, Jean (1509–64), *Commentarii in omnes epistolas Pauli apostoli* (Strasbourg: W. Rihel, 1539); *Opera quae supersunt omnia* (ed. W. Baum et al.; Braunschweig: C. A. Schwetschke, 1895), 52. 437–50; *Commentaries on the Epistles to Timothy, Titus, and Philemon* (Calvin's Commentaries 42; Grand Rapids, Mich.: Eerdmans, 1948) 345–61; *The Second Epistle of Paul the Apostle to the Corinthians and the Epistles to Timothy, Titus and Philemon* (Calvin's Commentaries, ed. D. W. Torrance and T. F. Torrance; Grand Rapids, Mich.: Eerdmans, 1964) 391–401.

Gérard, Andreas (1511–64), *Medulla omnium epistolarum Sancti Pauli et epistolarum canonicarum aliorum Sanctorum* (Lyons: A. Jullieron, 1672) 367–74.

Camerarius, Joachim (1500–74), *Commentarius in Novum Foedus: In quo et figurae sermonis, et verborum significatio, et orationis sententia, ad illius foederis intelligentiam certiorem, tractantur* . . . (Cambridge: R. Daniel, 1642).

Aretius, Benedictus (1505–74), *Commentarii in omnes epistolas d. Pauli et canonicas* . . . (Bern: J. de Preux, 1596) 398–404.

Bullinger, Heinrych (1504–75), *Commentarii in omnes Pauli Apostoli epistolas, atque etiam in Epistolam ad Hebraeos* . . . (Zurich: A. Cambiere, 1603) 487–90.

Daneau (Danaeus), Lambert (1530–95?), *Methodus sacrae Scripturae tractandae quae praxi, id est, aliquot exemplis et perpetuo in Epistolam Pauli ad Philemonem commentario illustrantur* (Geneva: P. Santandreanum, 1579).

Rollock, Robert (1555?–99), *In epistolam Pauli apostoli ad Thessalonicenses posteriorem commentarius . . . in epistolam Pauli apostoli ad Philemonem* (Edinburgh: Robert Charteris, 1598; Herbornae Nassauiorum, 1601).

Bèze, Théodore de (1519–1605), *Dn. nostri Iesu Christi Testamentum Novum* (London: Typographeum Regium, 1592) 167.

Estius, Gulielmus (Willem Hessels van Est) (1542–1613), *In omnes d. Pauli epistolas item in Catholicas* (3 vols.; Mainz: Kirchheim, 1858–59), 2. 858–67.

Dyke, Daniel (d. 1614), *Two Treatises: The One, a Most Fruitful Exposition upon Philemon; the Other, . . .* (London: Mylbourne, 1618).

Piscator, Johannes (1546–1625), *Analysis logica quinque nostremarum epistolarum Pauli videlicet Epistolae at Timotheum prioris, Timotheum posterioris, Titum, Philemonem, Hebraeos . . .* (Herborn: C. Corvini, 1592).

Crell, Johann (1590–1633), *Opera omnia exegetica* (4 vols. in 3; Amsterdam: Irenicus Philalethius, 1656), 2. 55–59.

Jones, William (1561–1636), *A Commentary upon the Epistles of Saint Paul to Philemon, and to the Hebrewes . . .* (London: R. Allot, 1635).

Balduinus, Fredericus, *Agenda apostolica cum intercessoriis pro impetranda servo converso . . . Hoc est, s. Apostoli Pauli epistolae ad Titum et Philemonem . . .* (Wittenberg: Helwigius, 1630).

Cornelius a Lapide (Cornelis Cornelissen van den Steen) (1567–1637), *Commentaria in omnes d. Pauli epistolas* (Antwerp: J. Meurs, 1665) 826–30.

Attersoll, William (d. 1640), *A Commentarie upon the Epistle of Saint Paul to Philemon . . .* (London: Wm. Iaggard, 1612; repr. London: T. Cotes, 1633).

Grotius, Hugo (Huig van Groot) (1583–1645), *Annotationes in Novum Testamentum* (2 vols.; Paris, 1644; editio nova, rev. C. E. de Windheim; vol. 1, Halle: Orphanotropheum, 1769; vol. 2, Erlangen: Ptochotrophium, 1757), 2. 831–38.

———, "Commentary on the Epistle of Paul the Apostle to Philemon," appended to *De jure belli ac pacis libri tres, in quibus ius naturae & gentium, item iuris publici praecipua explicatur* (Classics of Internationa Law; 2 vols.); vol. 1 (photographed Latin text; Washington, D.C.: Carnegie Institution of Washington, 1913) 612–18; vol. 2 (translation; Oxford: Clarendon, 1925) 865–75.

See W. Köhler, "Die Annotata des Hugo Grotius zum Philemonbrief des Apostels Paulus," *Grotiana* 8 (1940) 13–24.

Novarinus, A. (Luigi Novarini) (1594–1650), *Paulus expensus, notis, monitisque sacris . . .* (Verona: F. de Rubeis, 1644) 367–69.

Price, John (1600–76), *Commentarii in varios Novi Testamenti libros . . .* (London: J. Flesher, 1660).

Fell, John (1625–86), *A Paraphrase and Annotations upon All the Epistles of St. Paul* (1675; 3d ed., repr. London: R. Smith, 1702) 361–63.

Schmid, Sebastian (1617–96), *Epistola d. Pauli Apostoli ad Philemonem* (Strasbourg, 1691).

———, *In d. Pauli ad Colossenses epistolae commentatio . . . & ejus, quae ad Philemonem . . .* (Hamburg: B. Schiller, 1696).

Henry, Matthew (1662–1714), *Commentary on the Whole Bible in One Volume* (ed. L. F. Church; London: Marshall Morgan & Scott, 1960) 705–7.

———, "Philemon," *An Exposition of the Old and New Testament . . .* (London: S. Bagster, 1811), 6 (unpaginated).

Laurentii, Georg Michael (1670–1724), *Kurtze Erklärung des Briefs Pauli an die Thessalonicher . . . samt angehängter kurtzen Paraphrasi . . . des Briefs Pauli an Philemon* (2d ed.; Halle: Waysenhaus, 1714).

Bengel, Johann Albrecht (1687–1752), *Gnomon Novi Testamenti . . .* (Tübingen: J. H. P. Schramm, 1742) 888–90; *Gnomon of the New Testament: Now First Translated into English* (tr. A. R. Fausset; 5 vols.; Edinburgh: Clark, 1858); *Gnomon of the New Testament: A New Translation* (tr. C. T. Lewis and M. R. Vincent; 2 vols.; Philadelphia, Pa.: Perkinpine & Higgins, 1862); renamed and repr. *New Testament Word Studies* (Grand Rapids, Mich.: Kregel, 1971), 2. 566–69.

Calmet, Augustin (1672–1757), "Commentarius literalis in Ep. b. Pauli Apostoli ad Philemonem," *Commentarius literalis in omnes libros Novi Testamenti* (4 vols.; Würzburg: F. X. Rienner, 1788), 4. 308–15.

Wettstein, Johann Jakob (1693–1754), *Hē Kainē Diathēkē: Novum Testamentum graecum* (2 vols.; Amsterdam: Dommer, 1751–52), 2. 379–82.

Schmid, Lebrecht Christian Gottlob (1760–?), *Pauli Apostoli ad Philemonem epistola graece illustrata et ut exemplum humanitatis paulinae proposita* (Leipzig: Sommer, 1786).

Zachariae, Gotthilf Traugott (1727–77), *Kurze Erklärung der paulinischen Briefe an den Timotheus, Titus und Philemon . . .* (Göttingen: Kübler, 1774).

Lavater, J. C. (1741–1801), *Predigten über den Brief des heiligen Paulus an den Philemon* (Santgallen: Reutiner, 1785).

Storr, Gottlob Christian (1746–1805), *Opuscula academica ad interpretationem librorum sacrorum pertinentia* (2 vols.; Tübingen: J. G. Cotta, 1796), 2. 221–41.

Heinrichs, Johann Heinrich (1765–1850), *Pauli epistolae ad Timotheum, Titum et Philemonem . . .* (Novum Testamentum graece perpetua annotatione illustratum 3/1; Göttingen: Dietrich, 1783; repr. 1798, 1828).

D. Nineteenth- and Twentieth-Century Writers

(The more important commentaries are marked by an asterisk)

American Bible Union, *Notes on the Greek Text of the Epistle of Paul to Philemon . . .* (New York: American Bible Union, 1860).

Ash, A. L., *Philippians, Colossians & Philemon* (College Press NIV Commentary; Joplin, Mo.: College Press Publishing Co., 1994) 229–54.

Ashby, E. G., "The Letter to Philemon," *The New Layman's Bible Commentary* (ed. G. C. D. Howley et al.; Grand Rapids, Mich.: Zondervan, 1979) 1577–78; called in the U.K.: A *Bible Commentary for Today* (London and Glasgow: Pickering & Inglis, 1979) 1577–78.

Barclay, J. M. G., *Colossians and Philemon* (New Testament Guides; Sheffield, U.K.: Sheffield Academic, 1997) 97–126.

Barclay, W., *The Letters to Timothy, Titus, and Philemon: Revised Edition* (Daily Study Bible Series; Philadelphia, Pa.: Westminster, 1975) 267–83.

Barlow, G., "The Epistle of Paul to Philemon," *The Preacher's Complete Homiletic Commentary* . . . (32 vols.; ed. G. A. Barlow and R. Tuck; London and New York: Funk & Wagnalls, n.d.), 30. 105–14.

Barnes, A., *Notes on the New Testament* (Grand Rapids, Mich.: Kregel, 1962) 1202–12.

Bartina, S., *Epístola a Filemón* (La Sagrada Escritura, BAC 211; Madrid: Editorial Católica, 1962), 2. 1101–30.

Bartling, V. A., *Philemon* (Concordia Commentary; St. Louis, Mo.: Concordia Publishing House, 1970) 223–84.

Barton, B. B. et al., *Philippians, Colossians, Philemon* (Life Application Bible Commentary; Wheaton, Ill.: Tyndale House Publishers, 1995) 241–68.

Beet, J. A., A *Commentary on St. Paul's Epistles to the Ephesians, Philippians, Colossians, and to Philemon* (London: Hodder and Stoughton, 1890) 254–69.

*Benoit, P., *Les épîtres de Saint Paul aux Philippiens, à Philémon, aux Colossiens, aux Ephésiens* (SBJ; 3d ed.; Paris: Cerf, 1959) 39–46.

Bernard, D. K., *The Message of Colossians & Philemon* (Hazelwood, Mo.: Word Aflame, 1990) 149–84.

*Bieder, W., *Der Philemonbrief* (Prophezei; Zurich: Zwingli, 1944).

*Binder, H., *Der Brief des Paulus an Philemon* (THKNT 11/2; rev. J. Rohde; Berlin: Evangelische Verlagsanstalt, 1990).

Bisping, A., *Erklärung des zweiten Briefes an die Thessalonicher, der drei Pastoralen und des Briefes an Philemon* (Münster in W.: Aschendorff, 1858; 2d ed., 1865).

Blaiklock, E. M., *From Prison in Rome: Letters to the Philippians and Philemon* (London: Pickering & Inglis; Grand Rapids, Mich.: Zondervan, 1964) 71–72.

Bleek, F., *Vorlesungen über die Briefe an die Kolosser, den Philemon und die Ephesier* (ed. F. Nitzsch; Berlin: Reimer, 1865) 150–71.

Boise, J. R., *The Epistles of St. Paul Written after He Became a Prisoner* (New York: Appleton, 1887) 90–95.

Bouma, C., *De brief van den Apostel Paulus aan Filémon* (Korte verklaring der Heilige Schrift met nieuwe vertaling; Kampen: Kok, 1937; repr. 1953).

Bratcher, R. G., and E. A. Nida, *A Translators Handbook on Paul's Letters to the Colossians and to Philemon* (Helps for Translators 20; Stuttgart, London, and New York: United Bible Societies, 1977; repr. 1993) 111–33.

*Bruce, F. F., *The Epistles to the Colossians, to Philemon, and to the Ephesians* (NICNT 17; Grand Rapids, Mich.: Eerdmans, 1984) 189–225.

Bürki, H., *Der zweite Brief des Paulus an Timotheus, die Briefe an Titus und an Philemon* (Wuppertaler Studienbibel; Wuppertal: Brockhaus, 1975) 201–28.

Bynum, L., *Paul's Prison Letters* (Elgin, Ill.: Brethren, 1996) 48–53.

Caird, G. B., *Paul's Letters from Prison (Ephesians, Philippians, Colossians, Philemon) in the Revised Standard Version: Introduction and Commentary* (NClarB; Oxford: Oxford University, 1976; repr. 1981) 213–23.

Carson, H. M., *The Epistles of Paul to the Colossians and Philemon: An Introduction and Commentary* (TynNTC 12; Leicester, U.K.: Inter-Varsity; Grand Rapids, Mich.: Eerdmans, 1960; 7th ed., 1983; repr. 1984) 103–12.

Ceulemans, F. C., *Commentarius in epistolas s. Pauli* (3d ed.; Mechlin: Dessain, 1933) 221–28.

*Collange, J.-F., *L'Epître de Saint Paul à Philémon* (CNT 2/11c; Geneva: Labor et Fides, 1987).

Comblin, J., *Colosenses y Filemón* (Comentario bíblico ecuménico; Buenos Aires: La Aurora, 1989) 93–120.

Cosgrove, C. H., "Philemon," *Mercer Commentary on the Bible: Vol. 7, Acts and Pauline Writings* (Macon, Ga.: Mercer University, 1997) 285–91.

Cotrozzi, S., *Exegetischer Führer zum Titus- und Philemonbrief: Ein Wort-für-Wort-Überblick über sämtliche Auslegungs- und Übersetzungsvarianten* (Bonn: Kultur und Wissenschaft, 1998).

Cox, S., *The Epistle to Philemon* (2 vols. in 1; Minneapolis, Minn.: Klock & Klock Christian Publishers, 1867; repr. 1982).

Cserháti, S., *Pál apostolnak a Kolossébeliekhez írt levele és Filemonhoz írt levele* (Budapest: Magyarországi Evangélikus Egyház Sajtóosztálya, 1978) 177–212.

Davidson, F., et al., *The New Bible Commentary* (2d ed.; London: Inter-Varsity Fellowship, 1954) 1084–87.

Demme, J. I., *Erklärung des Briefes Pauli an Philemon* (Breslau, 1844).

*Dibelius, M., *An die Kolosser, Epheser, an Philemon* (HNT 12; 3d ed., rev. H. Greeven; Tübingen: Mohr [Siebeck], 1953) 101–8.

Dodd, C. H., "Philemon," *The Abingdon Bible Commentary* (ed. F. C. Eiselen et al.; New York: Abingdon, 1929) 1292–94.

Drysdale, A. H., *The Epistle of St. Paul to Philemon* (Devotional Commentary; London: Religious Tract Society, 1906; 3d ed., 1925).

*Dunn, J. D. G., *The Epistles to the Colossians and to Philemon: A Commentary on the Greek Text* (Carlisle, U.K.: Paternoster; Grand Rapids, Mich.: Eerdmans, 1996) 291–349.

Dunnam, M. D., *Galatians, Ephesians, Philippians, Colossians, Philemon* (The Communicator's Commentary 8; Waco, Tex.: Word Books, 1982) 405–17.

Eales, S. J., "The Epistle of Paul to Philemon," *The Pulpit Commentary* (ed. H. D. M. Spence and J. S. Exell; New York: A. D. F. Randolph, n.d.), 48. i–xi, 1–13.

Egger, W., *Galaterbrief, Philipperbrief, Philemonbrief* (2d ed.; Würzburg: Echter-V., 1988) 75–85.

Eisentraut, E., *Des heiligen Apostels Paulus Brief an Philemon: Eingehender Kommentar und zugleich Einführung in die Paulusbriefe* (Würzburg: C. J. Becker, 1928).

Ellicott, C. J., *Ellicott's Bible Commentary in One Volume* (Grand Rapids, Mich.: Zondervan, 1971) 1121–23.

———. A *Critical and Grammatical Commentary on St. Paul's Epistles to the Ephesians, Colossians and to Philemon* . . . (Boston, Mass.: Halliday, 1876) 275–78.

Ellis, D., "Commentary on the Book of Philemon," *The Randall House Bible Commentary* (Nashville, Tenn.: Randall House Publications, 1990) 411–44.

Ellis, E. E., "The Epistle to Philemon," *Wycliffe Bible Commentary* (ed. C. F. Pfeiffer and E. F. Harrison; Chicago: Moody, 1962) 889–93.

Elmore, V. O., *Exploring the Christian Way* (Nashville, Tenn.: Broadman, 1978).

Erdman, C. R., *The Epistles of Paul to the Colossians and to Philemon: An Exposition* (Philadelphia, Pa.: Westminster, 1933; repr. 1966) 125–52.

———, *Las epístolas a los Colosenses y a Filemón* (Grand Rapids, Mich.: T.E.L.L., 1976).

*Ernst, J., *Die Briefe an die Philipper, an Philemon, an die Kolosser, an die Epheser* (RNT; Regensburg: Pustet, 1974) 123–39.

Esser, J. P., *De brief aan Philemon* (Utrecht: Kemink en zoon, 1875).

Ewald, P., *Die Briefe des Paulus an die Epheser, Kolosser und an Philemon ausgelegt* (KNT 10; 2d ed.; Leipzig: Deichert, 1910) 262–85.

Fields, W., *Philippians—Colossians—Philemon: A New Commentary, Workbook, Teaching Manual* (Joplin, Mo.: College Press, 1969) 250–79.

Firminger, W. K., *The Epistles of St. Paul the Apostle to the Colossians and to Philemon with Introduction and Notes* (Indian Church Commentaries; London: SPCK, 1921).

Fitzmyer, J. A., *The Acts of the Apostles* (AB 31; New York: Doubleday, 1998).

———, "The Letter to Philemon," *JBC*, 2. 332–33 (art. 54).

———, "The Letter to Philemon," *NJBC*, 869–70 (art. 52).

———, "La lettera a Filemone," *Nuovo Grande Commentario Biblico* (ed. F. Dalla Vecchia et al.; Brescia: Queriniana, 1997) 1138–40 (art. 52).

———, "Carta a Filemón," *Comentario Bíblico "San Jerónimo"* (ed. R. E. Brown et al.; 5 vols.; Madrid: Cristiandad, 1972), 4. 203–6.

———, *Romans* (AB 33; New York: Doubleday, 1993).

Flatt, J. F. von, *Vorlesungen über die Briefe Pauli an die Philipper, Kolosser, Thessalonicher und an Philemon* (ed. C. F. Kling; Tübingen: L. F. Fues, 1829).

Francke (Franke), A. H., *Kritisch-exegetisches Handbuch über die Briefe Pauli an die Philipper, Kolosser und Philemon* (MeyerK 9; 5th ed.; Göttingen: Vandenhoeck & Ruprecht, 1886).

Friedrich, G., "Der Brief an Philemon," *Die Briefe an die Galater, Epheser, Philipper, Kolosser, Thessalonicher und Philemon* (NTD 8; 9th ed.; Göttingen: Vandenhoeck & Ruprecht, 1962) 186–94; (14th ed., 1976) 277–87; (17th ed., 1976) 188–96.

Furnish, V. P., "The Letter of Paul to Philemon," *Interpreter's Concise Commentary* (8 vols.; ed. C. M. Laymon; Nashville, Tenn.: Abingdon, 1971; repr. 1983), 7. 475–82.

Furter, D., *Les épîtres de Paul aux Colossiens et à Philémon* (Commentaire évangélique de la Bible 8; Vaux-sur-Seine: Edifac, 1987).

Garland, D. E., *Colossians and Philemon* NIV Application Commentary; Grand Rapids, Mich.: Zondervan, 1998) 293–375.

Getty-Sullivan, M. A., *Philippians and Philemon* (New Testament Message 14; Wilmington, Del.: Glazier; Dublin: Veritas, 1980) 75–89.

Giavini, G., *Gioia e libertà in Cristo: Le lettere di s. Paolo ai Filippesi e a Filemone* (Commenti al Nuovo Testamento; Turin: Elle di Ci, 1979) 57–74.

*Gnilka, J., *Der Philemonbrief* (HTKNT 10/4; Freiburg im B.: Herder, 1982).

González Ruiz, J. M., *San Pablo: Cartas de la cautividad: Traducción y comentario* (Christus hodie 1; Rome and Madrid: Ediciones Aldecoa, 1956) 297–312.

Goodier, A., *The Epistle of St. Paul to Philemon* (Westminster Version of the Sacred Scriptures, New Testament 3; 3d ed.; London: Longmans, Green, 1939) 206–8.

Gould, D., *Philippians, Colossians, Philemon* (Shepherd's Notes; Nashville, Tenn.: Broadman & Holman, 1997) 72–82.

Gray, C., *The Epistles of St. Paul to the Colossians and Philemon* (London: Lutterworth, 1948) 77–91.

Guthrie, D., "Philemon," *The New Bible Commentary Revised* (ed. D. Guthrie et al.; London: Inter-Varsity; Grand Rapids, Mich.: Eerdmans, 1970) 1187–90.

Hackett, H. B., *Notes on the Greek Text of the Epistle of Paul to Philemon* (New York: American Bible Union, 1860).

Hagenbach, K. R., *Pauli epistolae ad Philemonem interpretatio* (Basel: Schweighauser, 1829).

*Harrington, D. J., *Paul's Prison Letters: Spiritual Commentaries on Paul's Letters to Philemon, the Philippians, and the Colossians* (Hyde Park, N.Y.: New City, 1997) 16–28.

Harris, M. J., *Colossians & Philemon* (EGGNT; Grand Rapids, Mich.: Eerdmans, 1991) 239–88.

Harvey, H., *Commentary on the Pastoral Epistles, First and Second Timothy and Titus; and the Epistle to Philemon* (ACNT; Philadelphia, Pa.: American Baptist Publication Society, 1890) 151–64.

Haupt, E., *Die Gefangenschaftsbriefe* (MeyerK 9; 7th ed.; Göttingen: Vandenhoeck & Ruprecht, 1897; 8th ed., 1902) 189–212.

Havener, I., *First Thessalonians, Philippians, Philemon, Second Thessalonians, Colossians, Ephesians* (Collegeville Bible Commentary 8; Collegeville, Minn.: Liturgical, 1983) 45–50.

Hendriksen, W., *New Testament Commentary: Exposition of Colossians and Philemon* (Grand Rapids, Mich.: Baker Book House, 1964) 207–27.

Hofmann, J. C. K. von, *Die Briefe Pauli an die Kolosser und an Philemon* (Die heilige Schrift Neuen Testaments 4/2; Nördlingen: Beck, 1870) 193–218.

Houlden, J. L., *Paul's Letters from Prison: Philippians, Colossians, Philemon, and Ephesians* (Westminster Pelican Commentaries; Harmondsworth: Penguin; Philadelphia, Pa.: Westminster, 1970; repr. 1977) 223–32.

*Hübner, H., *An Philemon, an die Kolosser, an die Epheser* (HNT 12; Tübingen: Mohr [Siebeck], 1997) 25–39.

Huby, J., *Saint Paul: Les epîtres de la captivité* (VS 8; 2d ed.; Paris: Beauchesne, 1947) 115–26.

Ironside, H. A., *Addresses—Lectures—Expositions on Timothy, Titus and Philemon* (New York: Loizeaux Bros., 1947) 275–88.

Johnson, P. C., *The Epistle to Titus and Philemon: A Study Manual* (Grand Rapids, Mich.: Baker Book House, 1966).

Johnston, G., *Ephesians, Philippians, Colossians and Philemon* (CentB; London: Nelson, 1967) 71–80.

Jones, J. E., *A Commentary on the Epistle of Paul to Philemon* (Lousville, Ken.: Dissertation, Southern Baptist Seminary, 1949).

Kelly, W., *An Exposition of the Epistle of Paul to Titus and of That to Philemon, with Translation of an Amended Text* (London: Thomas Weston, 1901; repr. Oak Park, Ill.: Bible Truth Publications; Denver, Colo.: Wilson Foundation, 1968).

Ketter, P., *Die kleinen Paulusbriefe: Die Gefangenschaftsbriefe* (Die heilige Schrift für das Leben erklärt 15; Freiburg im B.: Herder, 1937) 200–15.

Knabenbauer, J., *Commentarius in S. Pauli epistolas: V. Epistolae ad Thessalonicenses, ad Timotheum, ad Titum et ad Philemonem* (Cursus Sacrae Scripturae, NT 2/5; Paris: Lethielleux, 1913) 375–91.

Knight, J. A., *Philippians, Colossians, Philemon* (Beacon Bible Expositions 9; Kansas City, Mo.: Beacon Hill, 1985) 259–84.

Knox, J., and G. A. Buttrick, "The Epistle to Philemon," *IB*, 11. 553–73.

Koch, A., *Commentar über den Brief Pauli an den Philemon . . .* (Zurich: Orell Füssli, 1846).

Koenig, J., *Galatians, Philippians, Philemon, Thessalonians* (ed. E. Krentz et al.; Augsburg Commentary on the New Testament; Minneapolis, Minn.: Augsburg, 1985) 183–208.

Kuschel, H. J., *Philippians, Colossians, Philemon* (Milwaukee, Wis.: Northwestern Publishing House, 1986) 210–18.

Leaney, A. R. C., *The Epistles to Timothy, Titus and Philemon: Introduction and Commentary* (Torch Bible Commentaries; London: SCM, 1960) 133–44.

Lee, W., *Paul's Epistles* (9 vols.; Anaheim, Calif.: Living Stream Ministry, 1984), 9.

Lehmann, R., *Epître à Philémon: Le christianisme primitif et l'esclavage* (Geneva: Labor et Fides, 1978).

Lenski, R. C. H., *The Interpretation of St. Paul's Epistles to the Colossians, to the Thessalonians, to Timothy, to Titus and to Philemon* (Columbus, Ohio: Lutheran Book Concern, 1937) 961–86.

Le Seur, P., *Die Briefe an die Epheser, Kolosser und an Philemon* (Bibelhilfe für die Gemeinde, NT 10; Leipzig: G. Schloessmann, 1936) 123–37.

*Lightfoot, J. B., *Saint Paul's Epistles to the Colossians and to Philemon* (London and New York: Macmillan, 1875; 9th ed., 1890) 299–344; reprinted many times, sometimes by different publishers.

———, *Colossians and Philemon* (Crossway Classic Commentaries; Wheaton, Ill., and Nottingham, U.K.: Crossway Books, 1994; repr. 1997) 127–42.

*Lohmeyer, E., *Die Briefe an die Philipper, an die Kolosser und an Philemon übersetzt und erklärt* (MeyerK 9; 13th ed.; Göttingen: Vandenhoeck & Ruprecht, 1964) 171–92; with Beiheft by W. Schmauch (1964) 86–98.

*Lohse, E., *Die Briefe an die Kolosser und an Philemon übersetzt und erklärt* (MeyerK 9/2; 14th ed.; Göttingen: Vandenhoeck & Ruprecht, 1968) 259–88; (15th ed., 1977).

———, *A Commentary on the Epistles to the Colossians and to Philemon* (Hermeneia; Philadelphia, Pa.: Fortress, 1971) 185–208.

Lowther Clark, W. K., *The Epistles of Paul the Apostle to the Ephesians, Philippians, Colossians and to Philemon* (Cambridge: Cambridge University, 1920).

Lueken, W., "Die Briefe an Philemon, an die Kolosser und an die Epheser," *Die Schriften des Neuen Testaments* . . . (2 vols.; 3d ed.; Göttingen: Vandenhoeck & Ruprecht, 1917), 2/2. 96–99.

MacArthur, J., *Colossians & Philemon* (Chicago: Moody, 1992) 201–35.

McDonald, H. D., *Commentary on Colossians & Philemon* (Theta Books; Waco, Tex.: Word Books, 1980) 149–94.

Maclaren, A., *Epistles of St Paul to the Colossians and Philemon* (Expositor's Bible; London: Hodder and Stoughton; New York: Armstrong, 1893; 9th ed., 1899).

Martin, E. D., *Colossians, Philemon* (Believers Church Bible Commentary; Scottsdale, Pa.: Herald, 1993) 239–79.

*Martin, R. P., *Colossians and Philemon* (NCentBC; London: Marshall, Morgan & Scott; Grand Rapids, Mich.: Eerdmans, 1973; repr. 1981) 143–70.

———, *Ephesians, Colossians, and Philemon* (Interpretation; Atlanta, Ga.: John Knox, 1991) 133–45.

Masini, M., *Filippesi—Colossesi—Efesini—Filemone: Le lettere della prigonia* (Leggere oggi la Bibbia 2/9; Brescia: Queriniana, 1987).

Matter, H. M., *De brief aan de Philippenzen en de Brief aan Philémon* (Commentaar op het Nieuwe Testament; Kampen: Kok, 1965).

Mayer, G., *Der Philemonbrief und die Petrusbriefe in religiösen Betrachtungen für das moderne Bedürfnis* (Gütersloh: Bertelsmann, 1910) 1–38.

Médebielle, A., "Epître à Philémon traduite et commentée," *PSB* 12 (Paris: Letouzey et Ané, 1951) 259–68.

Meinertz, M., and F. Tillmann, *Die Gefangenschaftsbriefe des heiligen Paulus übersetzt und erklärt* (Die Heilige Schrift des Neuen Testamentes 7; 4th ed.; Bonn: Hanstein, 1931) 107–20.

Melick, R. R., Jr., *Philippians, Colossians, Philemon* (The New American Commentary; Nashville, Tenn.: Broadman, 1991) 335–69.

Melsted, S., *Brjef Páls postula til Kólossaborgarsafnadar og til Fílemons* (Reykjavik: Prentad hjá Einari Thórdarsyni, 1882) 91–105.

Meyer, H. A. W., *Kritisch-exegetisches Handbuch über die Briefe Pauli an die Philipper, Kolosser und an Philemon* (MeyerK 9; 4th ed.; Göttingen: Vandenhoeck & Ruprecht, 1874).

———, *Critical and Exegetical Handbook to the Epistle to the Ephesians and the Epistle to Philemon* (Edinburgh: Clark, 1880) 355–83.

Morey, E. W., *Search the Scriptures: How to Study the Bible for Yourself: The Inductive Approach Applied to Philemon and Ephesians* (Vienna, Va.: Agape Ministry, 1993).

Morris, L., *1 and 2 Timothy, Titus, Philemon, Hebrews, James* (Bible Study Books; Grand Rapids, Mich.: Eerdmans, 1969) 32–34.

*Moule, C. F. D., *The Epistles of Paul the Apostle to the Colossians and to Philemon* (CGTC; Cambridge: Cambridge University, 1958) 140–49.

———, "Colossians and Philemon," *Peake's Commentary on the Bible* (ed. M. Black and H. H. Rowley; London: Nelson, 1962) 990–95, esp. 994–95.

Moule, H. C. G., *The Epistles of Paul the Apostle to the Colossians and to Philemon* (CBSC; Cambridge: Cambridge University, 1893; repr. 1932) 147–78.

Moulton, H. K., *Colossians, Philemon and Ephesians* (Epworth Preacher's Commentaries; London: Epworth, 1963) 69–75.

Müller, J. J., *The Epistles of Paul to the Philippians and to Philemon* (NICNT; Grand Rapids, Mich.: Eerdmans, 1955) 171–93.

Murphy-O'Connor, J., "Philemon," A *New Catholic Commentary on Holy Scripture* (ed. R. C. Fuller et al.; London: Nelson, 1969) 1218–19 (§929a–g).

Obiols, S., *Epistoles de Sant Pau* (La Biblia de Montserrat 21; Montserrat: Monestir de Montserrat, 1930).

O'Brien, P. T., *Colossians, Philemon* (WBC 44; Waco, Tex.: Word Books, 1982) 263–308.

Oesterley, W. O. E., "The Epistle of Paul to Philemon," *Expositor's Greek Testament* (5 vols.: London: Hodder and Stoughton, 1910–12), 4. 203–17.

Oltramare, H., *Commentaire sur les épîtres de s. Paul aux Colossiens, aux Ephésiens et à Philémon* (3 vols.; Paris: Librairie Fischbacher, 1891–92), 3. 437–67.

Oosterzee, J. J. van, *The Epistle of Paul to Philemon: A Theological and Homiletic Commentary* (A Commentary on the Holy Scriptures . . . NT 8; ed. J. P. Lange; New York: Scribner, Armstrong & Co., 1868; 3d ed., 1869) 1–31.

———, *Die Pastoralbriefe und der Brief an Philemon* (Theologisch-homiletisches Bibelwerk, NT 11; Bielefeld: Velhagen und Klasing, 1861; 2d ed., 1864) 143–55.

Parry, T., *Paul, Philemon, and Onesimus, Or Christian Brotherhood: Being a Practical Exposition of St. Paul's Epistle to Philemon* . . . (London: Rivington, 1834).

Patzia, A. G., *Colossians, Philemon, Ephesians* (San Francisco, Calif.: Harper & Row, 1984); repr. as *Ephesians, Colossians, Philemon* (New International Bible Commentary; Peabody, Mass.: Hendrickson, 1990) 103–17.

Peretto, E., *Lettere dalla prigionia: Filippesi—Colossesi—Efesini—Filemone* (Nuovissima versione della Bibbia dai testi originali 41; Rome: Edizioni Paoline, 1972) 77–90.

Petermann, J. H., *Pauli epistola ad Philemonem speciminis loco ad fidem versionum orientalium veterum una cum earum textu originali graece edita* (Berlin: Lüderitz, 1844).

Petersen, N. R., "Philemon," *Harper's Bible Commentary* (ed. J. L. Mays; San Francisco, Calif.: Harper & Row, 1988) 1245–48.

Radford, L. B., *The Epistle to the Colossians and the Epistle to Philemon with Introduction and Notes* (Westminster Commentaries; London: Methuen, 1931) 323–67.

Reapsome, M., *Colossians & Philemon: Finding Fulfillment in Christ: 10 Studies for Individuals or Groups* (Downers Grove, Ill.: InterVarsity, 1989).

Rees, P. S., *The Epistle to the Philippians, Colossians, and Philemon* (Proclaiming the New Testament; Grand Rapids, Mich.: Baker Book House, 1964) 125–40.

Rendtorff, H., "Der Brief an Philemon," *Die kleineren Briefe des Apostels* (NTD 8; 4th ed.; Göttingen: Vandenhoeck & Ruprecht, 1949) 153–57.

Reuss, J., *Die Briefe des Apostels Paulus: Timotheus, Titus, Philemon, Hebräer* (Echter-Bibel; 2d ed.; Würzburg: Echter-V., 1968) 47–50.

Richardot, M., *L'Epître à Philémon: Etude critique et exégétique* (Paris: Henri Jouve, 1894).

Riess, H., *Der Philemon-, Titus- und 2 Timotheusbriefe* (Christus heute 14; Stuttgart: Kreuz, 1956).

Robbins, R. F., "Philemon," *The Broadman Bible Commentary* (12 vols.; ed. C. J. Allen; Nashville, Tenn.: Broadman, 1969–72), 11. 377–88.

Roberts, J. H., *Die brief aan Filemon* (Kommentaar op die Nuwe Testament; Capetown, R.S.A.: Lux Verbi, 1992).

Roehrs, W., and M. Franzmann, *Concordia Self-Study Commentary* (Saint Louis, Mo.: Concordia, 1979) 231–32.

Rolston, H., "The Letter of Paul to Philemon," *The Layman's Bible Commentary* (25 vols.; ed. B. H. Kelly; Richmond, Va.: John Knox, 1959–63), 23. 124–31.

Rothe, M., *Pauli ad Philemonem epistolae interpretatio historico-exegetica* (Bremen, 1844).

Rupprecht, A. A., "Philemon," *The Expositor's Bible Commentary with the NIV* . . . (12 vols.; Grand Rapids, Mich.: Zondervan, 1978), 10. 135–48.

Sargent, J. E., *1 and 2 Timothy, Titus, and Philemon* (Cokesbury Basic Bible Commentary; Nashville, Tenn.: Graded Press, 1988) 137–56.

Saunders, E. W., *1 Thessalonians, 2 Thessalonians, Philippians, Philemon* (Knox Preaching Guides; Atlanta, Ga.: John Knox, 1981) 107–19.

Schlatter, A., *Die Briefe an die Galater, Epheser, Kolosser und Philemon ausgelegt für Bibelleser* (Erläuterungen zum Neuen Testament 7; Berlin: Evangelische Verlagsanstalt, 1953).

Scott, E. F., *The Epistles of Paul to the Colossians, to Philemon and to the Ephesians* (MNTC; 7th ed.; London: Hodder and Stoughton; New York: Harper and Bros., n.d.) 95–115.

Scroggie, W. G., *A Note to a Friend: Paul to Philemon* (London: Hulbert Publishing Co., 1927; repr. as *Studies in Philemon* (Grand Rapids, Mich.: Kregel, 1977, 1982).

Shearer, S., "The Epistle of St Paul to Philemon," *A Catholic Commentary on Holy Scripture* (ed. B. Orchard et al.; New York, Edinburgh, and Toronto: Nelson, 1953) 1152.

Smelik, E. L., *De brieven van Paulus aan Timotheüs, Titus en Filemon: De wegen der Kerk* (3d ed.; Nijkerk: Callenbach, 1961) 147–69.

Soden, H. von, *Die Briefe an die Kolosser, Epheser, Philemon; Die Pastoralbriefe* (HCNT 3/1; 2d ed.; Freiburg and Leipzig: Mohr [Siebeck], 1893) 73–78.

Sordi, M., *Paolo a Filemone o della schiavitù* (Università Cattolica di Milano, Ricerche dell'Istituto di Storia Antica 2; Milan: Jaca Book, 1987).

Staab, K., *Die Thessalonicherbriefe; Die Gefangenschaftsbriefe* (RNT 7/1; 5th ed.; Regensburg: Pustet, 1969) 106–13.

Steenkiste, J.-A. van, *Commentarius in omnes S. Pauli Epistolas ad usum seminariorum et cleri* (2 vols.; 6th ed.; Bruges: C. Beyaert, 1899), 2. 445–69.

*Stöger, A., *Der Brief an Philemon* (GSLNT 12/2; Düsseldorf: Patmos, 1965) 109–52.

*———, *The Epistle to Philemon* (NTSR 20/2; New York: Herder and Herder, 1971) 53–100.

*Stuhlmacher, P., *Der Brief an Philemon* (EKKNT 18; Einsiedeln: Benziger; Neukirchen-Vluyn: Neukirchener-V., 1975; 3d ed., 1989).

*Suhl, A., *Der Philemonbrief* (Zürcher Bibelkommentare NT 13; Zurich: Theologischer-V., 1981).

Thompson, G. H. P., *The Letters of Paul to the Ephesians, to the Colossians and to Philemon* (CBCNEB; Cambridge: Cambridge University, 1967) 173–92.

Vaughan, C., *Colossians and Philemon* (Bible Study Commentary; Grand Rapids, Mich.: Zondervan, 1973; repr. 1980) 119–33.

*Vincent, M. R., A *Critical and Exegetical Commentary on the Epistles to the Philippians and to Philemon* (ICC; New York: Scribner's Sons; Edinburgh: Clark, 1897; 5th ed., 1955) 155–94.

Vinet, A., *Etudes et méditations évangéliques: I. Epîtres aux Colossiens et à Philémon* (Lausanne: Payot, 1946).

Wall, R. W., *Colossians & Philemon* (IVP New Testament Commentary 12; Downers Grove, Ill., and Leicester, U.K.: InterVarsity, 1993) 179–218.

Walter, N., E. Reinmuth, and P. Lampe, *Die Briefe an die Philipper, Thessalonicher und an Philemon* (NTD 8/2; 18th ed.; Göttingen: Vandenhoeck & Ruprecht, 1998).

Weed, M. R., *The Letters of Paul to the Ephesians, the Colossians, and Philemon* (Living Word Commentary 11; Austin, Tex.: Sweet, 1971) 9–26.

Weiss, B., A *Commentary on the New Testament* (4 vols.; New York: Funk & Wagnalls, 1906), 4. 135–41.

Wette, W. M. L. de, *Kurze Erklärung der Briefe an die Colosser, an Philemon, an die Epheser und Philipper* (KEHNT 2/4; Leipzig: Weidmann, 1843).

Williams, A. L., *The Epistles of Paul the Apostle to the Colossians and to Philemon* (Cambridge Greek Testament for Schools and Colleges; Cambridge: Cambridge University, 1907) lxvi–lxxiv, 172–91.

Williams, D., and B. Gerrity, *Philemon* (2d ed.; Glendale, Calif.: GL Regal Books, 1979).

Williamson, J., *Discovering Timothy, Titus, and Philemon* (Guideposts Home Bible Study Program; Carmel, N.Y.: Guideposts Associates, 1986) 128–43.

Wohlenberg, G., *Die Briefe Pauli aus seiner ersten römischen Gefangenschaft* (Kurzgefasster Kommentar zu den heiligen Schriften des Alten und Neuen Testamentes, NTAbt. 4; Munich: Beck, 1895).

*Wolter, M., *Der Brief an die Kolosser; der Brief an Philemon* (ÖTBKNT 12; Würzburg: Echter-V.; Gütersloh: Mohn, 1993) 225–82.

*Wright, N. T., *The Epistles of Paul to the Colossians and to Philemon* (TynNTC 12; Leicester, U.K.: InterVarsity; Grand Rapids, Mich.: Eerdmans, 1986) 164–92.

Zedda, S., *Prima lettura di San Paolo: Introduzione, Analisi—Parafrasi, Note* (3 vols.; 3d ed.; Turin: Technograph, 1957–59), 1. 209–15.

II. Monographs

Barnett, A. E., *The Letters of Paul* (Nashville, Tenn.: Abingdon-Cokesbury, 1947) 157–60.

Baur, F. C., *Paulus, der Apostel Jesu Christi: Sein Leben und Wirken, seine Briefe und seine Lehre* (2 vols.; 2d ed., rev. E. Zeller; Leipzig: Fue's Verlag, 1866–67), 2. 88–94; *Paul, the Apostle of Jesus Christ: His Life and Work, His Epistles and His Doctrine* (2 vols.; London: Williams & Norgate, 1875–76), 2. 80–84.

Berger, A., *Encyclopedic Dictionary of Roman Law* (TAPS n.s. 43/2; Philadelphia, Pa.: American Philosophical Society, 1953).

Bjerkelund, C. J., *Parakalô: Form, Funktion und Sinn der parakalô-Sätze in den paulinischen Briefen* (Bibliotheca theologica norvegica 1; Oslo: Universitetsforlaget, 1967) 17–19, 52, 100, 119–24, 137, 167, 186.

Bright, L., "Philemon," *Paul II* (Scripture Discussion Commentary 11; Chicago: ACTA Foundation, 1971) 205–9.

Brown, R. E., *An Introduction to the New Testament* (ABRL; New York: Doubleday, 1997) 502–10.

Burtchaell, J. T., *Philemon's Problem: The Daily Dilemma of the Christian* (Chicago: ACTA Foundation, 1973); *Philemon's Problem: A Theology of Grace* (Grand Rapids, Mich.: Eerdmans, 1998) 5–16.

Callahan, A. D., *Embassy of Onesimus: The Letter of Paul to Philemon* (The New Testament in Context; Valley Forge, Pa.: Trinity Press International, 1997).

Campbell, J. Y., *Three New Testament Studies* (Leiden: Brill, 1965) 1–28.

Däberitz, A., *Der Brief an Philemon: 2 bibl. Szenen* (Dresden, 1927).

Debatin, H., *Der Brief an Philemon: Paulus bittet für den Sklaven Onesimus* (Amorbach, 1938).

De Wette, W. M. L., *An Historico-Critical Introduction to the Canonical Books of the New Testament* (Boston: Crosby Nichols and Co., 1858) 269–70.

Doty, W. G., *Letters in Primitive Christianity* (Guides to Biblical Scholarship; Philadelphia, Pa.: Fortress, 1973).

Earle, R., *Word Meanings in the New Testament: Volume 5, Philippians—Philemon* (Grand Rapids, Mich.: Baker, 1977) 269–72.

———, *Word Meanings in the New Testament, One-Volume Edition* (Grand Rapids, Mich.: Baker, 1986) 417–18.

Elmore, V. O., *Exploring the Christian Way* (Nashville, Tenn.: Broadman, 1978) 62–70.

Ernst, K. J., *The Art of Pastoral Counselling: A Study of the Epistle to Philemon* (Grand Rapids, Mich.: Zondervan, 1941).

Fernández, J., *La sociedad heril y la epístola de S. Pablo a Filemón* (Badajoz, 1946).

Gaebelein, F. E., *Philemon, the Gospel of Emancipation* (New York: Our Hope Press, 1939; repr. Wheaton, Ill.: Our Hope, Van Kampen, 1948).

González, J. L., *Tres meses en la escuela de la prisión: Estudios sobre Filipenses, Colosenses, Filemón y Efesios* (Nashville, Tenn.: Abingdon, 1997) 90–96.

Goodspeed, E. J., *The Meaning of Ephesians* (Chicago: University of Chicago, 1933).

———, *New Solutions to New Testament Problems* (Chicago: University of Chicago, 1927) 50–64.

Greeven, H., *Das Hauptproblem der Sozialethik in der neueren Stoa und im Urchristentum* (NTF 3/4; Gütersloh: Bertelsmann, 1935) 52–55.

Gromacki, R. G., *Stand Perfect in Wisdom: An Exposition of Colossians and Philemon* (Grand Rapids, Mich.: Baker Book House, 1981).

Guthrie, D., *New Testament Introduction: The Pauline Epistles* (London: Tyndale, 1961) 247–54.

Gutzke, M. G., *Plain Talk on Timothy, Titus and Philemon* (Grand Rapids, Mich.: Zondervan, 1978) 217–35.

Hainz, J., *Ekklesia: Strukturen paulinischer Gemeinde-Theologie und Gemeinde-Ordnung* (BU 9; Regensburg: Pustet, 1972) 199–209.

Hawkins, O. S., *Tearing Down Walls and Building Bridges* (Nashville, Tenn.: Thomas Nelson, 1995).

Hughes, R. K., *Colossians and Philemon: The Supremacy of Christ* (Westchester, Ill.: Crossway Books, 1989) 161–66.

Jang, L. K., *Der Philemonbrief im Zusammenhang mit dem theologischen Denken des Apostels Paulus* (Bonn: Dissertation, Universität Bonn, 1964).

Judge, E. A., *The Social Pattern of Christian Groups in the First Century* (London: Tyndale, 1960).

Kent, H. A., *Treasures of Wisdom: Studies in Colossians & Philemon* (Grand Rapids, Mich.: Baker Book House, 1978).

Knox, J., *Marcion and the New Testament: An Essay in the Early History of the Canon* (Chicago: University of Chicago, 1942).

Koester, H., *Introduction to the New Testament* (2 vols.; Philadelphia, Pa.: Fortress, 1982), 2. 134–35.

Kümmel, W. G., *Introduction to the New Testament: Revised Edition* (Nashville, Tenn., and New York: Abingdon, 1975) 348–50.

Lähnemann, J., and G. Böhm, *Der Philemonbrief: Zur didaktischen Erschliessung eines Paulusbriefes* (Handbücherei für den Religionsunterricht Heft 16; Gütersloh: Mohn, 1973).

Lappas, J., *Paulus und die Sklavenfrage: Eine exegetische Studie in historischer Schau* (Vienna: Dissertation, University of Vienna, 1954).

Loane, M. L., *Three Letters from Prison: Studies in Ephesians, Colossians and Philemon* (Waco, Tex.: Word Books, 1972) 121–34.

Lucas, R. C., *Fullness & Freedom: The Message of Colossians & Philemon* (Downers Grove, Ill.: InterVarsity, 1980) 181–91.

Lyall, F., *Slaves, Citizens, Sons: Legal Metaphors in the Epistles* (Grand Rapids, Mich.: Zondervan, 1984).

Martin, D. B., *Slavery as Salvation: The Metaphor of Slavery in Pauline Christianity* (New Haven, Conn.: Yale University, 1990).

Marxsen, W., *Introduction to the New Testament: An Approach to Its Problems* (Oxford: Blackwell; Philadelphia, Pa.: Fortress, 1968) 69–70.

Massini, M., *Filippesi—Colossesi—Efesini—Filemone: Le lettere della prigionia* (Brescia: Queriniana, 1987).

Mayser, E., *Grammatik der griechischen Papyri aus der Ptolomäerzeit* (2 vols.; 2d ed.; Berlin: de Gruyter, 1935–38).

Meeks, W. A., *The First Urban Christians: The Social World of the Apostle Paul* (New Haven, Conn.: Yale University, 1983) 59–60, 64.

Meinertz, M., *Der Philemonbrief und die Persönlichkeit des Apostles Paulus* (Düsseldorf: Schwann, 1921).

Metzger, B. M., *Index to the Periodical Literature on the Apostle Paul* (NTTS 1; Leiden: Brill, 1960) 126–27.

Michaelis, W., *Einleitung in das Neue Testament* (2d ed.; Bern: B. Haller, 1954) 261–65.

Moule, H. C. G., *Colossian and Philemon Studies: Lessons in Faith and Holiness* (London: Pickering & Inglis; Grand Rapids, Mich.: Zondervan, [1962]) 277–318.

———, *Studies in Colossians & Philemon* (Grand Rapids, Mich.: Kregel, 1977) 147–78.

O'Brien, P. T., *Understanding the Basic Themes of Colossians, Philemon* (Dallas, Tex.: Word Publishing, 1991) 91–104.

Ollrog, W.-H., *Paulus und seine Mitarbeiter: Untersuchungen zu Theorie und Praxis der paulinischen Mission* (WMANT 50; Neukirchen-Vluyn: Neukirchener-V., 1979) 101–6, 122–28.

Overbeck, F., *Studien zur Geschichte der alten Kirche* (1875; repr. Darmstadt: Wissenschaftliche Buchgesellschaft, n.d.) 158–230.

Pierson, R. H., *Love Come Home* (Washington, D.C.: Review and Herald Pub. Association, 1987) 101–8.

Prat, F., *The Theology of Saint Paul* (2 vols.; Westminster, Md.: Newman Bookshop, 1956), 1. 275–79.

Rapske, B. M., *The Book of Acts and Paul in Roman Custody* (The Book of Acts in Its First Century Setting 3; Carlisle, U.K.: Paternoster; Grand Rapids, Mich.: Eerdmans, 1994).

Sampley, J. P., *Pauline Partnership in Christ: Christian Community and Commitment in Light of Roman Law* (Philadelphia, Pa.: Fortress, 1980).

Saunders, E. W., *1 Thessalonians, 2 Thessalonians, Philippians, Philemon* (Knox Preaching Guides; Atlanta, Ga.: John Knox, 1981) 107–19.

Schenke, H.-M., and K. M. Fischer, *Einleitung in die Schriften des Neuen Testaments* (Berlin: Evangelische Verlagsanstalt, 1978) 154–57.

Schmid, J., *Zeit und Ort der paulinischen Gefangenschaftsbriefe* (Freiburg im B.: Herder, 1931).

Schnelle, U., *Einleitung in das Neue Testament* (UTB 1830; Göttingen: Vandenhoeck & Ruprecht, 1994) 173–82.

Schrage, W., *Die konkreten Einzelgebote in der paulinischen Paränese: Ein Beitrag zur neutestamentlichen Ethik* (Gütersloh: Mohn, 1961).

Schumann, A., *Paulus an Philemon: Betrachtungen zur Einführung in ein tieferes Verständnis des kleinsten Paulusbriefes und in die soziale Gedankenwelt des Neuen Testaments* (Leipzig: Hinrichs, 1908).

Staton, K., *Timothy—Philemon* (Standard Bible Studies; Cincinnati, Ohio: Standard Publishing, 1988) 195–206.

Thomas, W. H. G., *Studies in Colossians and Philemon* (Grand Rapids, Mich.: Kregel Publications, 1986) 139–65.

Townsend, J., *Colossians and Philemon: A Runaway Church and a Runaway Slave* (Elgin, Ill.: D. C. Cook, 1987) 108–26.

Vincent, M. R., *Word Studies in the New Testament* (4 vols.; New York: Scribner's Sons, 1901–5), 3. 515–26.

Wansink, C. S., *Chained in Christ: The Experience and Rhetoric of Paul's Imprisonment* (JSNTSup 130; Sheffield, U.K.: Sheffield Academic, 1996) 147–99.

Weima, J. A. D., *Neglected Endings: The Significance of the Pauline Letter Closings* (JSNTSup 101; Sheffield, U.K.: Sheffield Academic, 1994) 230–36.

Wikenhauser, A., and J. Schmid, *Einleitung in das Neue Testament* (6th ed.; Freiberg im B.: Herder, 1973) 475–79.

Wiles, G. P., *Paul's Intercessory Prayers: The Significance of the Intercessory Prayer Passages in the Letters of St Paul* (SNTSMS 24; Cambridge: Cambridge University, 1974) 281–84.

Wright, N. T., *The Climax of the Covenant: Christ and the Law in Pauline Theology* (Minneapolis, Minn.: Fortress, 1991) 49–54.

III. Articles

Anon., "Carta a Filemón," *CB* 10 (1953) 34–36.

Anon., "The Epistle to Philemon: An Expanded Paraphrase," *EvQ* 34 (1962) 221–22.

Anon, "Philemon," *Cyclopaedia of Biblical, Theological and Ecclesiastical Literature* (12 vols.; ed. J. M'Clintock and J. Strong; New York: Harper & Bros., 1879; repr. Grand Rapids, Mich.: Baker Book House, 1970), 8. 82–85.

Allen, D. L., "The Discourse Structure of Philemon: A Study in Textlinguistics," *Scribes and Scriptures: New Testament Essays in Honor of J. Harold Greenlee* (ed. D. A. Black; Winona Lake, Ind.: Eisenbrauns, 1992) 77–96.

Allevi, L., "Il cristianesimo e la schiavitù nella lettera a Filemone," *ScCatt* 6/10 (1927) 415–29.

Baljon, J. M. S., "Opmerkingen op het gebied van de Conjecturaalkritiek: De brief aan Titus en de brief aan Philemon," *ThStud* 8 (1890) 118–24, esp. 122–24.

Balz, H., "Philemonbrief," *TRE* 26 (1996) 487–92.

Barclay, J. M. G., "Paul, Philemon and the Dilemma of Christian Slave-Ownership," *NTS* 37 (1991) 161–86.

Bartchy, S S., "Philemon, Epistle to," *ABD*, 5. 305–10.

Bartina, S., "Filemón, Epístola a," *Enciclopedia de la Biblia* (6 vols.; ed. A. Díez Macho et al.; Barcelona: Garriga, 1963–65), 3. 540–43.

Barton, S., "Paul and Philemon: A Correspondence Continued," *Theology* 90 (1987) 97–101.

Bergh van Eysinga, G. A. van den, "De brief aan Philemon," *Nieuw theologisch Tijdschrift* 29 (1940) 1–18.

Bouwman, G., "Philemon" and "Philemonbrief," *Bibel-Lexikon* (ed. H. Haag; Einsiedeln: Benziger, 1968) 1376.

Bover, J. M., "El 'sentido social' de las epístolas de San Pablo," *RF* 114 (1938) 323–40.

Caldwell, E., "The Ideal Brother: A Book Study of Philemon," *USR* 27 (1915–16) 139–43.

Callahan, A. D., "Brother Love," *Harvard Divinity Bulletin* 22/4 (1993) 11, 14–16.

Cladder, H. J., and H. Dieckmann, "Der Brief an Philemon: Zum Seelenbild des hl. Paulus," *Katholische Gedanke* 2 (1929) 342–65.

Daube, D., "Onesimus," *HTR* 79 (1986) 40–43.

Demarest, J. K., "The Epistle to Philemon," *LQ* 20 (1890) 514–23.

Dennison, J. T., Jr., "Paul, Philemon, Onesimus and the New Creation in Christ Jesus," *Kerux* 6/3 (1991) 38–45.

Derrett, J. D. M., "The Functions of the Epistle to Philemon," *ZNW* 79 (1988) 63–91.

Díaz Mateos, M., " 'La solidaridad de la fe': Eclesiología de la carta a Filemón," *Paginas* 15/101 (1990) 23–39.

Diem, H., "Onesimus—Bruder nach dem Fleisch und in dem Herrn: Die Botschaft des Apostels Paulus an Philemon in ihrer dauernden Aktualität," *Evangelische Freiheit und kirchliche Ordnung* (ed. W. Metzger et al.; Stuttgart: Steinkopf, 1968) 139–50.

Dittberner, A., "Paul and Philemon," *TBT* 95 (1978) 1578–82.

Dodd, C. H., "The Mind of Paul: Change and Development," *BJRL* 18 (1934) 69–110; repr. in his *New Testament Studies* (Manchester: Manchester University, 1953) 83–128.

Dormeyer, D., "Flucht, Bekehrung und Rückkehr des Sklaven Onesimos: Interaktionale Auslegung des Philemonsbriefes," *Der evangelische Erzieher* 35 (1983) 214–28.

Elliott, J. H., "Patronage and Clientism in Early Christian Society," *Forum* 3/4 (1987) 39–48.

Elliott, J. K., "A Greek-Coptic (Sahidic) Fragment of Titus-Philemon (0205)," *NovT* 36 (1994) 183–95.

Feeley-Harnik, G., "Is Historical Anthropology Possible? The Case of the Runaway Slave," *Humanizing America's Iconic Book: Society of Biblical Literature Centennial Addresses 1980* (Biblical Scholarship in North America 6; ed. G. M. Tucker and D. A. Knight; Chico, Calif.: Scholars, 1982) 95–126.

Fransen, I., "L'Appel d'un coeur sincère (Lettre à Philémon)," *BVC* 39 (1961) 32–36.

Galán, A., "¿Tomó San Pablo de la religiones místicas sus ideas de manumisión cristiana?" *RF* 49 (1917) 141–52.

Galassi, J., "The Epistle of Paul to Philemon: A Prisoner of Christ," *Incarnation: Contemporary Writers on the New Testament* (ed. A. Corn; New York: Viking, 1990) 257–64.

Garofalo, S., "Del sentire cristiano: La lettera di S. Paolo a Filemone," *Humanitas* 1 (1946) 20–29.

Gaulmyn, M. M. de, "Réflexion sur l'Epître de Paul à Philémon: Proposition de lecture présentée par un groupe de Lyon," *Sémiotique et Bible* 11 (1978) 7–25 or 18–23.

Getty, M. A., "The Letter to Philemon," *TBT* 22 (1984) 137–44.

———, "The Theology of Philemon," SBLSP 1987 (ed. K. H. Richards; Atlanta, Ga.: Scholars, 1987) 503–8.

Godet, F., "The Epistle to Philemon: The Oldest Petition for the Abolition of Slavery," *Expos* 3/5 (1887) 138–54.

Groupe de Montpellier, "L'Epître de Paul à Philémon," *Sémiotique et Bible* 11 (1978) 7–17.

Hackett, H. B., "Philemon" and "Philemon, The Epistle of Paul to," *A Dictionary of the Bible . . .* (3 vols.; ed. W. Smith; Boston: Little, Brown and Co., 1863), 2. 831–33.

Hahn, F., "Paulus und der Sklave Onesimus: Ein beachtenswerter Kommentar zum Philemonbrief," *EvT* 37 (1977) 179–85.

Hall, B. G., "Philemon and Slavery," *ExpTim* 41 (1929–30) 336.

Harrison, P. N., "Onesimus and Philemon," *ATR* 32 (1950) 268–94.

Hemer, C. J., "Philemon, Epistle to," *The International Standard Bible Encyclopedia* (4 vols.; ed. G. W. Bromiley; Grand Rapids, Mich.: Eerdmans, 1979–88), 3. 831–32.

Herranz, A., "De sociología cristiana," *EstBíb* 2 (1931) 264–69.

Hill, A. D., "Christian Character in the Marketplace: Colossians, Philemon and the Practice of Business," *Crux* 30/2 (1994) 27–34.

Hooker, M. D., "Interchange in Christ," *JTS* 22 (1971) 349–61.

Hulsebos, J., "De brief van Paulus aan Filémon," *GTT* 3 (1902) 5–7, 17–19, 35–39.

Imschoot, P. van, "L'Epître à Philémon," *Collationes gandavenses* 14 (1927) 170–76.

Jeremias, J., "Chiasmus in den Paulusbriefen," *ZNW* 49 (1958) 145–56.

Jones, J. E., "The Letter to Philemon—an Illustration of Koinonia," *RevExp* 46 (1949) 454–66.

Kallemeyn, H., "Philémon et son prochain," *Revue Reformée* 46 (1995) 15–18.

Karrer, M., "Philemonbrief," *EKL* 3 (1992) 1180.

Kea, P. V., "Paul's Letter to Philemon: A Short Analysis of Its Value," *PRS* 23 (1996) 223–32.

Keulenaer, J. de, "De epistola S. Pauli ad Philemonem," *Collationes Mechlinenses* 11 (1937) 484–91.

Knight, E. F., "The Reception of Onesimus by Philemon," *ExpTim* 28 (1916–17) 92.

Koch, E. W., "A Cameo of Koinonia: The Letter to Philemon," *Int* 17 (1963) 183–87.

Lähnemann, J., "Der Philemonbrief," *Hochschuldidaktische Materialien* 39 (1973) 51–87.

Légasse, S., "L'Epître à Philémon," *CahEv* n.s. 33 (1980) 51–62.

Lewis, L. A., "An African American Appraisal of the Philemon-Paul-Onesimus Triangle," *Stony the Road We Trod: African American Biblical Interpretation* (Minneapolis, Minn.: Fortress, 1991) 232–46.

Llewelyn, S. R., "The Crucifixion of a Slave" and "The Government's Pursuit of Runaway Slaves," *NDIEC* 8 (1997–98) 1–3 and 9–46.

Lock, W., "The Epistle to Philemon," *Theology* 15 (1927) 159–61.

Losada, D. A., "Para una introducción a la lectura de la Carta a Filemón," *RevistB* 43 (1981) 193–216.

Lührmann, D., "Wo man nicht mehr Sklave oder Freier ist," *WD* n.s. 13 (1975) 53–83.

Lyman, M. E., "Philemon, Letter to," *IDB*, 3. 782–84.

Maclaren, A., "The Epistle to Philemon," *Expos* 3/5 (1887) 270–82, 363–75, 443–53; 3/6 (1887) 150–59, 180–91, 297–306.

Mayer, B., "Paul's Letter to Philemon, a Model for Exegesis," *Henceforth, Journal for Advent Christian Thought* 11 (1983) 95–106.

Michel, O., "Philemon, Philemonbrief," *Calwer Bibellexikon* (5th ed.; ed. T. Schlatter et al.; Stuttgart: Calwer V., 1959) 1030–31.

Migliazza, B. L., "Text Analysis Observations from Philemon Using Fleming's Stratificational Model," *Notes on Translation* 2/4 (1988) 36–48.

Motyer, S., "The Little Epistles of the New Testament: Philemon," *Evangel* 4/4 (1986) 2–6.

Mulholland, D. M., "Enfrentando injustiças: Estudo baseado em Filemom," *Vox Scripturae* 2 (1992) 55–66.

Müller-Bardorff, J., "Philemonbrief," *RGG*[3] 5 (1961) 331–32.

Murphy-O'Connor, J., "The Christian and Society in St Paul," *New Blackfriars* 50 (1968–69) 174–82.

Olinger, D., "A Redemptive-Historical Consideration of Philemon," *Kerux* 12/1 (1997) 23–32.

Patzia, A., "Philemon, Letter to," *Dictionary of Paul and His Letters* (ed. G. F. Hawthorne and R. P. Martin; Leicester, U.K., and Downers Grove, Ill.: InterVarsity, 1993) 703–7.

Pommier, J., "Autour du billet à Philémon," *RHPR* 8 (1928) 180–81.

Preiss, T., "Life in Christ and Social Ethics in the Epistle to Philemon," *Life in Christ* (SBT 13; London: SCM, 1954) 32–42.

———, "Vie en Christ et éthique sociale dans l'Epître à Philémon," *Aux sources de la tradition chrétienne: Mélanges offerts à M. Maurice Goguel . . .* (Bibliothèque théologique; Neuchâtel and Paris: Delachaux & Niestlé, 1950) 171–79; repr. *La vie en Christ* (Neuchâtel and Paris: Delachaux & Niestlé, 1951) 65–73.

Reid, J., "The Message of the Epistles: Philemon," *ExpTim* 45 (1933–34) 164–68.

Rhijn, C. H. van, "De jongste literatuur over de Schriften des Nieuwen Verbonds: De brief aan Philémon," *ThStud* 5 (1887) 356–59.

Richardson, W. J., "Principle and Context in the Ethics of the Epistle to Philemon," *Int* 22 (1968) 301–16.

Roberts, J. H., "Die brief aan Filemon: Bevryding en christelike verantwoordelikheid," *TheolEv* 18/3 (1985) 19–26.

———, "Filemon in diskussie: Enkele hoogtepunte in die stand van sake," *Scriptura* 21 (1987) 24–50.

———, "Navorsingsberig: 'n kommentaar, Filemon en Kolossense," *TheolEv* 22/3 (1989) 14–20.

———, "Teologie en etiek in die brief aan Filemon: 'n poging tot verantwording," *Skrif en Kerk* 14 (1993) 105–15.

Robertson, A. T., "Philemon and Onesimus: Master and Slave," *Expos* 8/19 (1920) 29–48.

Rollins, W. G., "Philemon, Letter to," *IDBSup*. 663–64.

———, "Slavery in the NT," *IDBSup*, 830–32.

Russell, D. M., "The Strategy of a First-Century Appeals Letter: A Discourse Reading of Paul's Epistle to Philemon," *Journal of Translation and Textlinguistics* 11 (1998) 1–25.

Sampley, J. P., "Societas Christi: Roman Law and Paul's Conception of the Christian Community," *God's Christ and His People: Studies in Honour of Nils Alstrup Dahl* (ed. J. Jervell and W. A. Meeks; Oslo: Universitetsforlaget, 1977) 158–74.

Scarpat, G., "La 'lettera a Filemone' ed il pensiero di Paolo sulla schiavitù," *Il pensiero di Paolo nella storia del cristianesimo antico* (Pubblicazioni dell'Istituto di Filologia Classica e Medievale 82; ed. A. Ceresa-Gastaldo; Genoa: Università di Genova, 1983) 57–79.

Schmauch, W., "Philemonbrief," *EKL* (4 vols.; ed. H. Brunotte and D. Weber; 1956–61), 3. 183.

Schmitz, J. R., "Generativity in the Letter to Philemon," *Emmanuel* 91 (1985) 156–60.

Scott, C. A., "The Epistle to Philemon," *Expos* 8/2 (1911) 328–37.

S. E. C. T., "The Atonement—an Illustration," *Expos* 1/9 (1879) 221–33.

Snyman, A. H., "A Semantic Discourse Analysis of the Letter to Philemon," *Text and Interpretation: New Approaches in the Criticism of the New Testament* (NTTS 15; ed. P. J. Hartin and J. H. Petzer; Leiden: Brill, 1991) 83–99.

Soards, M. L., "Benefitting from Philemon," *Journal of Theology* (United Theological Seminary) 91 (1987) 44–51.

Soesilo, D., "The Story Line in Translating Philemon," *BT* 34 (1983) 424–26.

Sohn, O. E., "The Forgotten Epistle," *CTM* 20 (1949) 13–29.

Sousa, J. de, "Filemón," *Enciclopedia de la Biblia* (6 vols.; ed. A. Díez Macho et al.; Barcelona: Garriga, 1963–65), 3. 538–39.

Steensgaard, P., "Erwägungen zum Problem Evangelium und Paränese bei Paulus," *ASTI* 10 (1975–76) 110–28.

Steyn, G. J., "Some Figures of Style in the Epistle to Philemon: Their Contribution towards the Persuasive Nature of the Epistle," *Ekklesiastikos Pharos* 77 (1995) 64–80.

Suhl, A., "Der Philemonbrief als Beispiel paulinischer Paränese," *Kairos* 15 (1973) 267–79.

Troupeau, G., "Une ancienne version arabe de l'Epître à Philémon," *Mélanges offerts à M. Maurice Dunand* (= *MUSJ* 45–46; Beirut: Imprimerie Catholique, 1969–71), 2. 341–51.

Tuting, W. C., St. Paul's Epistle to Philemon: Slavery," *ExpTim* 40 (1928–29) 563.

Vassall-Phillips, O. R., "The Epistle to Philemon: An Echo from the Past," *Clergy Review* 2 (1931) 502–12.

Verdam, P. J., "St-Paul et un serf fugitif (Etude sur l'épître à Philémon et le droit)," *Symbolae ad jus et historiam antiquitatis pertinentes Julio Christiano van Oven dedicatae (Symbolae van Oven)* (ed. M. David et al.; Leiden: Brill, 1946) 211–30.

Vicentini, J. I., "¿Pablo revolucionario? Pero ¿Como? La esclavitud según la carta a Filemón," *RevistB* 32 (1971) 43–54.

Wiggers, J., "Beiträge zur Einleitung in die Briefe des Paulus an die Epheser, an die Kolosser und an den Philemon," *TSK* 14 (1841) 413–56, esp. 442–50.

Wilson, A., "The Pragmatics of Politeness and Pauline Epistolography: A Case Study of the Letter to Philemon," *JSNT* 48 (1992) 107–19.

Wright, N. T., "Putting Paul Together Again: Toward a Synthesis of Pauline Theology (1 and 2 Thessalonians, Philippians, Galatians, and Philemon)," *Pauline Theology, Volume I: Thessalonians, Philippians, Galatians, Philemon* (ed. J. M. Bassler; Minneapolis, Minn.: Fortress, 1991) 183–211.

Translation, Commentary, and Notes

◆

I. Prescript and Greeting (1–3)

[1]Paul, a prisoner for Christ Jesus, and Timothy, our brother, to Philemon, our dear friend and fellow worker, [2]to Apphia, our sister, to Archippus, our fellow soldier, and to the church at your house, [3]grace and peace to you from God our Father and the Lord Jesus Christ.

COMMENTS

Paul begins this brief letter as he has begun other letters, naming himself and the cosender, Timothy, and the addressees in the first two verses, and then adding his initial greeting (v 3). Such a three-part prescript was commonly used in contemporary ancient Greek letters: Sender to Addressees, with Greetings (see Fitzmyer, *NJBC*, art. 45, §8–9). Paul uses this prescript in what seems to be a very personal letter, but that prescript makes it likely that the letter was not intended to be read silently by those addressed, but to be read aloud to an assembled group of Christians. Although the letter itself is primarily addressed to Philemon, the addressees also include Apphia, who may be Philemon's wife or sister, Archippus, whose relation to Philemon or Apphia is not explained, and "the church at your house," which is a way of referring to Christians who were wont to gather at Philemon's house for liturgical services. The addressees are greeted as Christians, as the different epithets used of them reveal. The greeting of "grace and peace" is directed to all of them and strikes the chord of graciousness that pervades this letter.

The inclusion of Apphia, Archippus, and the house-church means that this is hardly a private letter, as J. Müller-Bardorff would have it (*RGG*^{3}, 5. 331–32); similarly Lightfoot (*Colossians and Philemon*, 301: a "strictly private letter"); Caird (*Paul's Letters*, 218). Paul is concerned that the whole community that gathers in prayer at Philemon's house be involved in the way Onesimus is to be welcomed back by Philemon. This concern thus gives to the Letter to Philemon a dimension that transcends that of private correspondence. See U. Wickert, "Der Philemonbrief." This has to be recognized even if, once the prescript comes to an end, one hears no more in the letter about the house-church. For Paul is trying to get Philemon to recognize the symbolic integrity of that congregation, which is made up of brothers and sisters who go beyond the intimate family or household of Philemon.

The use of the second singular predominates throughout the letter, and occasionally one encounters the singular vocative *adelphe* (vv 7, 20), addressed obviously to Philemon. Only toward the end of the letter does one find the second plural again (vv 22b, 25). This change from singular to plural within the same letter finds a parallel in *P. Giss. I* §54, sent *kyri[ō] mou timōtatō adelphō Olympiodōrō kai Hermaeiōni*, "to my lord, (my) most honored brother Olympiodorus, and to Hermaeion," in which the majority of the message is addressed in the singular to Hermaeion, but also with an instruction to Olympiodorus to help him. The letter closes with greetings for both addressees (see O. Eger et al., *Griechische Papyri im Museum des oberhessischen Geschichtsvereins zu Giessen* [Leipzig and Berlin: Teubner, 1910–12]).

Paul does not identify himself here, as he does in other letters when he wants to speak with authority, as an "apostle" (so in Rom 1:1; 1 Cor 1:1; 2 Cor 1:1; and especially in Gal 1:1)—a status for which he had to contend in the early church. Wickert, who rightly insists that this letter is not a private letter and that Paul is not writing as a private individual, nevertheless goes too far when he insists that Paul presents himself as an apostle and is asserting his authority to make Philemon accede to his plea (*ZNW* 52 [1961] 232–34). That view counters the rhetorical thrust of this letter, and especially what Paul explicitly says in vv 8–9.

Nor does he use "slave of Jesus Christ" (as in Rom 1:1; cf. Phil 1:1), probably because that term might have been too indelicate in this letter in view of the topic that it addresses. Rather, Paul chooses to mention only his condition as a "prisoner for Christ Jesus," and he writes this plea addressed to Philemon as one manacled. Although Timothy is mentioned as the cosender of the letter, this status of imprisonment is expressed in the singular, and so it applies solely to Paul. Such a description of himself is modified by some copyists of different MSS of this letter (see NOTE below). In the course of the letter Paul will depict himself as an elderly man (v 9), a father to Onesimus (v 10), a prisoner (v 10), a brother of Onesimus (v 16), a partner of Philemon (v 17), and a guest soon-to-be (v 22).

Paul sends his greetings of "grace and peace," as he customarily does in other letters, and stresses the source of those blessings as coming from "God our Father and the Lord Jesus Christ." This greeting as well as the concluding wish (v 22b), the final greeting (v 25), and the blessing are directed to all the addressees, whereas the main message in the body of the letter, and even in v 23, concerns only Philemon. That does not mean, however, that what is said to him should not be of concern to all the members of the congregation that meets at his house.

The prescript thus gives the reader a view of early Christian house-churches. The head of the house is recognized as the leader of such a church or congregation. Philemon, however, is not to be thought of as an absolute monarch, who may disregard what others might think. So the relation of the slave Onesimus to him becomes the concern of the church as well.

NOTES

1. *Paul.* The Apostle does not send this letter alone, as appears from the rest of this verse, where Timothy is mentioned as the cosender.

Greek *Paulos* is the only name that the Apostle uses of himself in his uncontested letters or that is used of him in the Deutero-Paulines and the Pastorals. It is also found in 2 Pet 3:15. *Paulos* is the Greek form of a well-known Roman name, *Paul(l)us,* which was the cognomen used by various *gentes*, the Aemilii, Sergii, Vettenii, and others (see F. Münzer, "Paullus," *PW* 18/4. 2362–63). This Roman name is the only thing in Paul's writings that supports the Lucan identification of the Apostle as a Roman citizen (Acts 16:37; 22:25–29; 23:27). Paul himself never mentions his Roman citizenship or his native origin in Tarsus of Cilicia (Acts 9:11; 11:25; 21:39; 22:3), citizens of which enjoyed Roman *civitas* (see Fitzmyer, *Acts*, 427–28). In the Letter to the Philippians, Paul tells of himself: "circumcised on the eighth day, of the people of Israel, of the tribe of Benjamin, a Hebrew born of Hebrews; as to the law a Pharisee, as to zeal a persecutor of the church, as to righteousness under the law blameless" (3:5–6).

Paul never says anything in his letters about his name *Saulos*, "Saul." If we were left only with the Pauline corpus, we would never know about it. For Luke alone among NT writers mentions it (Acts 7:58; 8:1, etc.; cf. especially 13:9, *Saulos ho kai Paulos,* "Saul, also known as Paul"). Luke also uses the Greek transliterated form *Saoul* (Acts 9:4, 17; 22:7, 13; 26:14), the Semitic form that appears in the accounts of Paul's call on the road to Damascus. It stands for Hebrew *Šāʾûl,* which means "asked for" (i.e. the child requested of God). It was the name of the great king of undivided Israel (1 Sam 9:2, 3, 5). *Saulos ho kai Paulos* reflects the custom of ancient Jews having two names, one Semitic and one Greek or Roman. "Paul" would have been his *cognomen,* and "Saul" his Semitic *signum* or *supernomen* (see further *PAHT*, 2 [§P3]; Fitzmyer, *Acts*, 502–3). Jerome, however, thought that "Paul" was adopted by Saul of Tarsus from the name of Sergius Paulus, the Roman proconsul of Cypriot Paphos, "the first spoils of the Church" there, once he had been converted to Christianity (*In Ep. ad Philemonem* 1 [PL 26. 640–41]).

prisoner for Christ Jesus. Paul identifies himself only as *desmios Christou Iēsou*, "a prisoner of Christ Jesus." The phrase is also found in Eph 3:1 and is imitated in the apocryphal *Letter of Paul to the Corinthians* 51.17 (M. Testuz, *Papyrus Bodmer X–XII* [Cologny-Geneva: Bibliothèque Bodmer, 1959] 32) and often in patristic writings (e.g. Epiphanius, *Panarion* 74.5.10 [CGS 37. 320]; *Ancoratus* 68.8 [GCS 25.84]; Eusebius, *Historia ecclesiastica* 6.11.5; *Comm. in Ps.* 69 [PG 23.764C]).

Paul does not mean thereby that he has been imprisoned by Christ, *pace* Soards ("Some Neglected Theological Dimensions," 213), but rather that he is imprisoned because of his relation to Christ Jesus. Unfortunately, he never explains the reason for the imprisonment in which he finds himself; nor does he mention the place where he had been imprisoned or by whom he has been imprisoned. In 2 Cor 11:23 he boasts only of having suffered "far more imprisonments" than others who have considered themselves apostles. Only in v 13 does he state that his present incarceration is related to his preaching of the gospel. As in Phil 1:7, 16, he means that what he has been doing in the evangelization of Gentiles has resulted in his condition as *desmios*, "someone bound, imprisoned." He thus appeals to Philemon, not as an apostle (as in 2 Cor 1:1; Gal 1:1), but as one in a lowly condition in order to support the appeal that he will make of him in vv 9–10; cf. vv 13, 23.

As a Roman citizen, Paul would not have been kept in harsh confinement; it was rather what is called *custodia libera* (liberal detention), and that is why he, even as a prisoner, can write to Philemon. See further B. Rapske, *The Book of Acts and Paul in Roman Custody*, 28, 32–34, 358. Paul does not mention his imprisonment in order to stir up mercy toward either himself or Onesimus, but at most to stress the lowly condition in which he is currently confined. Cf. Eph 3:1; 2 Tim 1:8.

MS D reads *apostolos* instead of *desmios*, and the minuscule MS 629 reads both *apostolos* and *desmios*; some minuscule MSS (323, 945) even read *doulos*, "slave," instead of *apostolos*. These are all scribal harmonizations with other letters, perhaps intended by copyists to tone down Paul's description of himself as *desmios*.

Some commentators (e.g. Stuhlmacher, *Brief an Philemon*, 30) have understood Paul's self-description as *desmios* in a figurative case, as in 2 Cor 2:14, maintaining that Paul was not really imprisoned when he wrote this letter. Similarly, Goodenough (*HTR* 22 [1929] 182–83). That, however, is a far-fetched understanding of what is written here, and especially of vv 13 and 22. Given that Paul mentions his imprisonment not only here but also in Phil 1:7, the mention of his status has to be taken at face value. Caird (*Paul's Letters*, 218) takes the phrase in both senses, as a prisoner for Christ's sake and also as Christ's prisoner, as does Houlden (*Paul's Letters*, 228).

The double name *Christos Iēsous* occurs again in vv 9 and 23. It is a Pauline favorite, often used in his uncontested letters (1 Thess 5:18; Gal 2:4, 16; 3:14, 26, 28; 4:14; 5:6, 24; 1 Cor 1:1, 2, 4, 30; 4:15, 17; 15:31; 16:24; 2 Cor 1:1; Phil 1:1, 6, 8, 26; 2:5; 3:3, 8, 12, 14; 4:7, 19, 21; Rom 2:16; 3:24; 6:3, 11, 23; 8:1, 2, 11, 34, 39; 15:5, 16, 17; 16:3) and imitated in the Deutero-Paulines (e.g. Col 1:1; Eph 1:1) and Pastoral Epistles (e.g. Titus 1:4; 1 Tim 1:1; 2 Tim 1:1). It is found a few times in Acts too (3:20; 5:42; 18:5, 28; 24:24), but nowhere else in the NT. The titular sense of *Christos*, "Anointed One, Messiah," appears in Rom 9:5, but *Christos* has otherwise become Jesus' second name, *Iēsous Christos*, which Paul likes to invert, as he does here. At times he also uses

Iēsous Christos, "Jesus Christ" (e.g. Gal 1:1, 12; 1 Cor 2:2; 8:6; 2 Cor 1:3; 13:5; Rom 1:8; 5:15; Phlm 3).

Timothy, our brother. Lit. "Timothy, the brother," i.e. fellow Christian, who is the cosender of this letter. He also appears as cosender in 1 Thess 1:1; Phil 1:1; in the Deutero-Pauline Col 1:1; 2 Thess 1:1 he is likewise so depicted.

The term *adelphos* clearly does not bear the meaning of blood brother or sibling; nor does it express a fictive kinship, for Paul means it in a real sense, because it describes one who shares the same condition, viz. being a Christian, or one born of a common regeneration and sharing the Christian destiny. That meaning of *adelphos* is found often in Acts (e.g. 1:15, 16; see NOTE in Fitzmyer, *Acts*, 222), and especially in Paul's letters (e.g. 1 Cor 1:1; 6:6; 8:12; 16:12; Rom 14:10, 13, 15; 16:23). The distinctive aspect of this status for Paul is seen in Rom 8:29, where he speaks of the risen Christ as *prōtotokon en pollois adelphois*, "firstborn among many brothers." In 1 Cor 5:11, however, Paul warns Corinthians that they should not associate with anyone, "if, bearing the name brother (*ean tis adelphos onomazomenos*), he is guilty of immorality or greed, is an idolator, reviler, drunkard, or robber." Hence *adelphos* and *adelphē*, "brother" and "sister," became the equivalent of *Christianos* and *Christianē*.

By so describing Timothy, Paul is alluding also to his trustworthiness as a fellow worker and to his valued service, which he lauds extensively in Phil 2:19–24. This also means that Timothy is aware of the issue about which Paul writes in this letter, and he lends his support to Paul's appeal. Presumably, Timothy had already made the acquaintance of Philemon, perhaps at the time of the latter's conversion in Ephesus, and that is why he is mentioned now as cosender. Jerome thought that Timothy's name was added so that the letter would have more authority (*In Ep. ad Philemonem* 1 [PL 26. 643]). Harris rightly insists that Timothy is not to be regarded "as a coauthor" of the letter (*Colossians & Philemon*, 244), for though Timothy is mentioned as the cosender, Paul continues in v 4 with the singular, "I give thanks." Hence Paul is the one who composes the letter.

Because Timothy is mentioned as a cosender of the letter, one must conclude that he had some access to the imprisoned Paul and thus became aware of Paul's writing. The same would have to be said of those mentioned in vv 23–24. Perhaps they were able to care for Paul in some way during his *custodia libera* (liberal detention). There is no indication that Paul dictated this letter to Timothy, *pace* Getty ("Theology," 504).

In Acts 16:1–3 Luke recounts how Timothy, the son of a Jewish woman and a Greek father, became Paul's coworker; he is said there to have been circumcised at Paul's desire so that he could assist in the evangelization of Jews. Moreover Luke tells especially of Timothy's cooperation with Paul during the latter's rather lengthy ministry in Ephesus (Acts 19:1–19), and even how Paul sent Timothy with Erastus to Macedonia (19:22). Timothy becomes in time the addressee of two of the Pastoral Letters in the Pauline corpus. In 2 Tim 1:5 Timothy's faith is compared to that of his grandmother Lois and his mother, Eunice. So that information helps to fill out the identification of the cosender of this letter. See further Fitzmyer, *Acts*, 574–75.

Philemon. He is the prime recipient of this Pauline letter, even though others are mentioned as addressees; he is the first named as such and is regarded by Paul as the *paterfamilias.* The name "Philemon" tells us unfortunately little about the background of this addressee. In the letter itself, Philemon appears as a young, well-to-do, respected Christian citizen of a Phrygian town, undoubtedly Colossae (see Introduction §15). He is probably the leader of the Christians of Colossae who meet as a congregation at his house.

Philēmōn is a Greek name, related to the verb *philein,* "love," and it probably meant something like "kindly, affectionate," or perhaps "worthy of love." Paul is possibly playing on the meaning of the name in using the modifying adjective *agapētos* (see next NOTE). The name *Philēmōn* was relatively common in Phrygia and is found in various inscriptions and papyri (see MM, 670; *NDIEC,* 3. 91; 5. 144); it also occurs in Aristophanes, *Birds* 763.

Philemon bears the name of a famous character in Greek mythology, which relates him to the Phrygian peasant couple Philemon and Baucis. In the legend, when Zeus and Hermes came to earth to test the piety of human beings, they were refused hospitality by all but the two aged Phrygians, Philemon and his wife. Then the gods revealed themselves to them and counseled Philemon and Baucis to climb a mountain, whence they saw the whole area beneath them covered by a flood. The pair then became priest and priestess to the gods, and eventually they were turned into beautiful trees. See Ovid, *Metamorphoses* 8.611–724.

Lightfoot understood Philemon to be the husband of Apphia and father of Archippus (*Colossians and Philemon,* 301, 304); see below. In later church legends Philemon became a bishop of Colossae (*Apostolic Constitutions* 7.46).

our dear friend. Lit. "the beloved one." Although Paul never uses *philos,* "friend," in this letter, he uses the adjective *agapētos,* which is employed elsewhere when he speaks of Christian fellow workers, collaborators, or acquaintances to whom he sends greetings (1 Cor 10:14; 15:58; 2 Cor 7:1; 12:19; Phil 2:12; 4:1; Rom 1:7; 16:5, 8, 9, 12), either in opening or closing salutations. According to Jerome, *agapētos* meant someone who deserved to be loved, *diligibilis,* and not only *dilectus.* Here it denotes Paul's affection for Philemon, whom he so addresses, because he was involved in his becoming a Christian (see v 20). Its connotation could also be "one loved by God or Christ" rather than loved by Paul, but the latter cannot be excluded; hence my translation. MS D adds *adelphō,* "(beloved) brother," which would again be meant in the figurative sense of "Christian." The addition, however, is suspect, because it looks like a scribal change in imitation of *adelphon agapēton* of v 16. See further O. Wischmeyer, "Das Adjektiv *agapētos.*"

fellow worker. Lit. "our fellow worker," because the pronoun *hēmōn* is found with this noun; but it is to be taken with the foregoing description *agapētō* as well. Paul uses the plural "our," meaning that Philemon was a collaborator of Timothy and himself. It does not emerge in this letter in what way or where Philemon was such a collaborator, but *synergos* would mean that somehow Philemon was involved personally in evangelical or church work, and specifically in Paul's evangelization of an area of Asia Minor, perhaps in Ephesus. Paul uses *synergos* similarly for several other persons who actively shared in his evangelical work: Timothy in 1 Thess 3:2; Rom 16:21; Titus in 2 Cor 8:23; Prisca and Aquila in Rom 16:3; Urbanus in Rom 16:9; Epaphroditus in Phil 2:25; Clement in Phil 4:3. See also Col 4:11. Contrast the use of *koinōnos,* "partner," in v 17 below. Paul seems never to have visited Colossae; at least he never gives the impression that he has visited it in any of his letters.

2. *Apphia, our sister.* Lit. "the sister." The letter is sent also to a Christian woman, who is otherwise unknown, but addressed simply as *Apphia tē adelphē.* The appositive *adelphē* is the feminine counterpart of *adelphos,* used of Philemon in v 1 (see NOTE there), hence a Christian "sister" to Paul (as my translation has taken it). This is the reading of MSS א, A, D*, F, G, P, 048, 33, 81 1739, 1818; but MSS D[2], Ψ, and most minuscules read rather *agapētē,* "beloved Apphia," a suspect scribal change made to agree with the *agapētos* of v 1. MS 629, and some ancient versions combine the two adjectives, reading *adelphē tē agapētē,* "beloved sister."

Since the name "Apphia" follows that of Philemon, she may be his wife, as Chrysostom, Theodoret, Lightfoot, Caird, Carson, Gnilka, Lohse, Stuhlmacher, and many other commentators have interpreted the name. A few commentators, however, think rather that she was Philemon's sister (so Kümmel). In any case, as the lady of the house, she would have had to deal constantly with the household slaves (Friedrich, NTD[9], 189; NTD[14], 281). In accordance with his general understanding of this letter, Knox even considers Apphia to be possibly the wife of Archippus (*Philemon among the Letters,* 65 n. 5).

"Apphia" is a well-attested Phrygian female name (MM, 73), a form of which even appears on a Greek funerary inscription from Colossae, which reads: *Hermas A[p]phiadi / tē idiāi gynaika / tēi Tryphōnos / thygatri, genei / Kolossēnēi / [mnēm]ēs heneka,* "Hermas for Apphia, his wife, daughter of Trypho, a Colossian by birth: In [memo]ry!" (*CIG,* 3. 1168 [§4380k[3]]; cf. Dibelius, *An Philemon,* 111). There it does not refer to the same person as the one addressed in this letter. Grotius ("Commentary," 867) once claimed that her name was Roman (= Appia), with the *pi* changed to a *phi.* Lightfoot (*Colossians and Philemon,* 304–5) calls that analysis "a mistake," but Gnilka (*Philemonbrief,* 16) thinks otherwise. Compare BDR §42.3.

Pace Winter ("Paul's Letter," 2), there is not a hint here that *adelphē* means that Apphia was "also a church leader"; such a meaning of *adelphē* is nowhere attested.

Archippus. This is most likely the same person as the one mentioned in Col 4:17, where he is recognized as a follower of Epaphras, the evangelist of the Lycus Valley in Asia Minor, and is given the instruction "See that you fulfill the ministry that you have received in the Lord." Just what that *diakonia* would be is not explained there. It seems to refer to some important office that Archippus was holding, possibly the diaconate or a post of even greater importance in the church at Colossae. Subscriptions found at the end of the Greek text of the Letter to Philemon in some MSS (L, P) call Archippus a "deacon of the church in Colossae" (see NOTE on them at the end or *TCGNT*, 589–90). John Chrysostom regarded Archippus as one of the clergy (PG 62. 705). Ambrosian Hilary (on Col 4:17) thought that he became the successor of Epaphras as bishop of Colossae; similarly Jerome (*In Ep. ad Philemonem* 1 [PL 26. 642]). In *Apostolic Constitutions* 7.46 he is mentioned as a bishop of Laodicea. Caird, following Lohmeyer, considers him as a replacement for Epaphras during the latter's absence in Rome (*Paul's Letters*, 214).

Even though it is not said here, Archippus could be the son of Philemon and Apphia, as Theodore of Mopsuestia (PG 66. 950), Schlatter, Lightfoot, and others have understood it, but there is no certainty about that relationship, as was evident centuries ago. John Chrysostom considered Archippus to be merely *heteron tina isōs philon*, "someone else like a friend" of Paul (*Hom. 1 in Ep. ad Philemonem* [PG 62. 704]). Either meaning would explain why he has been included among the addressees. The following epithet given to him may even suggest that Archippus was a prominent member of the house-church that met at Philemon's residence.

Despite allegations to the contrary (like those of Knox, Cope, Winter), there is no reason to regard Archippus as Onesimus' master, or to think that the *diakonia* of Col 4:17 had anything to do with Onesimus. Moreover it is unlikely that he would be addressed here, along with Philemon and Apphia, if Philemon were living in another town (Laodicea), as Knox would have had it (see Introduction §20–24).

our fellow soldier. Or "comrade in arms" (NEB). *Systratiōtēs hēmōn* does not tell us on what campaign Archippus might have served together with Paul (and Timothy) as soldiers, and so it is probably only another (metaphorical) way of saying "our fellow worker" and hinting at its arduous task. The term is used in the NT elsewhere only of Epaphroditus in Phil 2:25, where Paul joins it with *synergos*, "fellow worker," a joining that is found also in Eusebius, *Comm. in Isaiam* 63.11.11 (GCS 9. 87). Such a joining is blithely passed over by Knox (*Philemon among the Letters*, 67). Elsewhere Paul uses the cognate noun *strateia*, "campaign" (2 Cor 10:4), and the verb *strateuesthai*, "serve as a soldier" (1 Cor 9:7; 2 Cor 10:3), in a metaphorical sense to describe arduous

Christian missionary endeavors. O. Bauernfeind, however, contends that the Pauline use of such terms to designate Christian ministry is "unusual" and believes that "the word group is not really at home in the vocabulary of Paul's letters" (*TDNT*, 7. 710–11). Compare 2 Tim 2:3. *Pace* Winter ("Paul's Letter," 2), the term is not used for "someone who gives aid, particularly financial." That would be a far-fetched meaning of the word.

and to the church at your house. Lit. "and the church according to your (singular) house," i.e. the church in Colossae. As Jerome noted, "your" is ambiguous, because it might refer to either Archippus or Philemon; but he also rightly argued that it should be understood of Philemon's house, to whom the letter itself is directed (*In Ep. ad Philemonem* 2 [PL 26. 644]). The singular *sou* is to be understood as referring to Philemon, the first named among the addressees, and not to Archippus, even though he is "the person named nearest this decisive phrase," as Knox claims (*Philemon among the Letters*, 62). Archippus only seems to be the "nearest available antecedent" of the pronoun *sou*, because the construction actually distinguishes Archippus, another addressee along with Apphia, from the person mentioned by *sou*. Moreover Paul takes it for granted that his letter would be read aloud to all of the Christians who meet in the house. This part of the verse shows that the Letter to Philemon was indeed a church letter, but that does not justify the thesis of E. J. Goodspeed (*New Solutions of New Testament Problems* [Chicago: University of Chicago, 1927] 51–61) that this letter was originally entitled *To the Laodiceans*, a thesis that Knox discusses (*Philemon among the Letters*, 93–94).

In the phrase *hē kat' oikon ekklēsia* the word *oikos* is likewise ambiguous. It could mean either "(according to your) household," i.e. the church made up of members of the household or family of Philemon, or it could refer to the physical "house," in which the family and other Colossian Christians met for liturgical and social services, i.e. a house-church. The latter is more likely, because there is evidence of early Christians meeting and praying in private houses (Acts 2:46; 5:42; 12:12), and one reads of *domus ecclesiae* in Christian writings of later date (see Lightfoot, *Colossians and Philemon*, 241). Moreover Paul himself uses the phrase elsewhere in the latter sense (1 Cor 16:19; Rom 16:5 [both referring to the house of Prisca and Aquila]); cf. Col 4:15 (house of Nympha at Laodicea); see further Fitzmyer, *Romans*, 736; Stuhlmacher, *Brief an Philemon*, 70–75 ("Exkurs: Urchristliche Hausgemeinden"). John Chrysostom considered it indicative of Philemon's character that he would have Christians of Colossae meet in his house (*In Ep. ad Philemonem*, Arg. [PG 62. 702]).

As Filson has noted ("Significance"), the house-church enabled the early followers of Jesus to have a distinctively Christian worship and a place for cultic activity. Although early Christians are depicted in Acts as going to the Temple at hours of prayer (2:46; 3:1), the time came when their cultic celebrations (especially that of the Lord's Supper) had to be carried out elsewhere. It was enacted then in the family life of a household, which at times was even converted en masse (Acts 16:33). The house-church grew out from there and included others, thus providing fellowship and the grouping of Christians, and in time even factions among them. When the Christians preached or proclaimed their faith, that was done often enough in public, and sometimes in stoas or halls (see Rordorf, "Was wissen," 115); but they gathered for common prayer in places set apart. This gave rise to the use of houses for such a purpose. The house-church came to represent a "cross section of society" and led eventually to the development of a distinctive church polity and structure. There is no evidence, however, of a separate building reserved for liturgy in the Roman empire before the third century A.D. Thus the house-church was a distinctively early Christian cultic creation. In mentioning the house-church, Paul brings the Christian congregation that meets in Philemon's house into concern for the object of his letter.

This is the only place where *ekklēsia* is mentioned in this letter, but it is a word that occurs forty-four times in Paul's uncontested letters and that forms an important part in his theology; in the Deutero-Paulines it is found fifteen times, and three times in the Pastorals. Here it denotes a small local organized Christian community of Colossae, of a size that could meet in Philemon's house. It does not have yet the connotation of a universal church, as do some passages in 1 Corinthians (or in Colossians and Ephesians). See further *PAHT*, 95–97 (§PT133–37).

3. *grace and peace to you.* This is Paul's standard epistolary greeting to his addressees, which he substitutes for the conventional secular epistolary greeting, *chairein,* which is found in Acts 15:23; 23:26; Jas 1:1. The Pauline greeting also occurs in 1 Thess 1:1; Gal 1:3; 1 Cor 1:3; 2 Cor 1:2; Phil 1:2; Rom 1:7; cf. 2 Thess 1:2; Col 1:2; Eph 1:2; Rev 1:4; but note the modification of it with the insertion of *eleos,* "mercy," in some of the Pastorals (1 Tim 1:2; 2 Tim 1:2). Paul thus greets Philemon and the others (the "to you" is plural) with the wish that they all will have a share in God's favor or grace and the peace that is derived from it.

"Grace" denotes the divine favor by which Christians are saved, and Paul wishes that all the addressees will have their due share of it, not relying on their own deeds or merits. "Peace" is not merely an inner composure of the undisturbed human spirit, because it echoes the OT *šālôm,* the meaning of which is expressed in the root *šlm,* "be complete, full, perfect," connoting the fullness of God's gracious bounty and that by which Christians are reconciled to God (see Rom 5:1–2). The Pauline greeting may also echo the priestly blessing of the sons of Aaron (Num 6:24–26): "May the Lord bless you and keep you; may the Lord make His face shine upon you and be gracious to you; may the Lord look kindly upon you and give you peace." As Rom 5:1 shows, "peace" is the lot of Christians who live in God's grace, and in Gal 5:22 it is listed among the fruits of the Spirit and expresses "peace with God, the benefits of salvation, harmony with all people" (*TLNT*, 1. 434). See further Fitzmyer, *Romans*, 228. To call this epistolary greeting "liturgical language," as does Getty ("Theology," 504), is a misuse of the term "liturgical."

from God our Father and the Lord Jesus Christ. The source of the "grace and peace" is double. Paul prays that both God and Christ will bestow this blessing on Philemon and the others. By "God the Father" the Christian Paul thus acknowledges not only Yahweh, the God of the OT, but also His fatherhood in a special way. In the OT God is called often the Father of corporate Israel (Deut 32:6; Isa 63:16; 64:8; Jer 3:4, 19; 31:9; Mal 2:10; Sir 51:10), because He was perceived as the creator and provider of His people. Now Paul speaks of God as the Father of Christians, as in Gal 1:3, 1 Cor 1:3; 2 Cor 1:2; Phil 1:2; Rom 1:7b.

Paul acknowledges that the risen Christ is equally the source of such blessing. He thus puts the risen Christ on the same level as God the Father, recognizing them both as the source of the grace and peace in his greeting. "God and Christ issue grace and peace to Philemon and others in the context of the human social world" (Soards, "Some Neglected Theological Dimensions," 214).

The title *Kyrios* is used of Christ, which denotes his status as the risen Lord; see further Fitzmyer, *Romans*, 112–13; *EDNT*, 2. 328–31. For the combination "Lord Jesus Christ," see also 1 Thess 1:1; 5:23; Gal 1:3; 6:18; Rom 5:1, 21. Calling Jesus Christ *Kyrios* in this letter is particularly significant, because as a common noun the word denotes "lord, master" and was particularly used in the contrast of *kyrios* and *doulos*, "master" and "slave," in the social world of the time. Recall how Paul describes a slave who has become a Christian as *apeleutheros Kyriou*, "a freedman of the Lord" (1 Cor 7:22).

BIBLIOGRAPHY

Banks, R., *Paul's Idea of Community: The Early House Churches in Their Historical Setting* (Exeter, U.K.: Paternoster; Grand Rapids, Mich.: Eerdmans, 1980) 33–42.

Elliot, J. H., "Philemon and House Churches," *TBT* 22 (1984) 145–50.

Filson, F. V., "The Significance of the Early House Churches," *JBL* 58 (1939) 105–12.

Galley, H. D., "Das 'Haus' im Neuen Testament," *Evangelisch-Lutherische Kirchenzeitung* 15 (1961) 201–5.

Hainz, J., *Ekklesia: Strukturen paulinischer Gemeinde-Theologie und Gemeinde-Ordnung* (BU 9; Regensburg: Pustet, 1972) 199–203.

Klauck, H. J., *Hausgemeinde und Hauskirche im frühen Christentum* (SBS 103; Stuttgart: Katholisches Bibelwerk, 1981) 41–44.

Malherbe, A. J., "House Churches and Their Problems," *Social Aspects of Early Christianity* (Baton Rouge, La.: Louisiana State University, 1977) 60–91.

Petersen, J. M., "House-Churches in Rome," *VC* 23 (1969) 264–72.

Rordorf, W., "Was wissen wir über die christlichen Gottesdiensträume der vorkonstantinischen Zeit?" *ZNW* 55 (1964) 110–28.

Wickert, U., "Der Philemonbrief—Privatbrief oder apostolisches Schreiben?" *ZNW* 52 (1961) 230–38.

Wischmeyer, O., "Das Adjektiv *agapētos* in den paulinischen Briefen: Eine traditionsgeschichtliche Miszelle," *NTS* 32 (1986) 476–80.

II. THANKSGIVING (4–7)

[4]I give thanks to my God, as I always remember you in my prayers, [5]because I hear about the faith that you have in the Lord Jesus and your love for all God's dedicated people, [6]so that the sharing in your faith may be effective in the realization of all the good that is ours in Christ. [7]For I have experienced much joy and consolation in your love, because the hearts of God's dedicated people have been refreshed through you, my brother.

COMMENTS

As in several of the letters to his churches, Paul in the second part of this letter gives thanks to God for Philemon's faith and love (4–7), about which he may have heard from Onesimus himself. The thanksgiving is not formulated as coming from Paul and Timothy; nor does it refer to all those named in vv 1–2. Rather Paul gives thanks for what he has heard about Philemon. This thanksgiving resembles the epistolary section of other letters (1 Thess 1:2–5; Phil 1:3–11; 1 Cor 1:4–8; Rom 1:8; cf. Col 1:3–8) and other Greek and Jewish letters from the third century B.C. on (e.g. *P. Hibeh* 79 [*kai tois theois pollē cha[ri]s*]; *P. Lond.* 42.1–10 [LCL: *Select Papyri*, 1. 283]; 1 Macc 12:11; 2 Macc 1:3–6). For Schubert and O'Brien, the thanksgiving would be limited to vv 4–6 (see Introduction §66).

This thanksgiving contains the ideal four elements of such a syntactical period in the Pauline letters, according to the analysis of Schubert: (1) the principal verb, *eucharistō*, "I give thanks"; (2) a temporal participle in the nominative, expressing a reason for the prayer of thanks, *mneian poioumenos*, "remembering"; (3) a causal participle stating the cause of Paul's prayer, i.e. his knowledge based on a report that he has had, *akouōn*, "hearing"; and (4) a final clause, expressing the content of the prayer, *hopōs*, "so that." It also sets up "the epistolary situation," introducing a "vital theme of the letter" (Schubert, *Form and Function*, 65–66, 180). It mentions themes that Paul will play on in the body of the letter or at its conclusion. Strikingly, however, it makes no mention of a runaway slave. This may, of course, be a delicate omission on Paul's part, but it may also alert the reader to the nature of the occasion of Paul's writing of this letter.

Mullins counts nine themes that are mentioned in the verses of the thanksgiving: *agapē* (love), *pistis* (faith), *ho kyrios Iēsous* (the Lord Jesus), *hagioi*

(God's dedicated people), *koinōnia* (sharing), *agathon* (the good), *chara* (joy), *paraklēsis* (consolation); all but four of them *(pistis, hagioi, chara, paraklēsis)* reappear later in the letter. These themes he compares with those in Colossians ("The Thanksgivings").

Even though Paul has mentioned Timothy as the cosender of the letter, he now gives thanks alone, as he prays to "my God" and recognizes what Philemon's faith and love have accomplished. Paul's language in these verses is epistolary, not liturgical. Using choice rhetorical phrases, he praises Philemon for what he has learned about his conduct and life. Significantly, Paul joins "faith" and "love," implying the relation of the latter to the former, as the relation of these two notions is expressed in Gal 5:6: "faith working itself out through love." Philemon is thus an example of such Christian faith. Paul himself will exploit this reference to Philemon's love when he appeals to him in v 9 "out of love."

To the prayer of thanksgiving (vv 4–5) Paul joins one of petition (v 6), that Philemon's faith may be effective in the realization of the bounty of being a Christian. Finally (v 7), in addition to his prayer of thanksgiving and petition, Paul expresses his own joy at the effects of Philemon's love, which has influenced both him and other Christians. Paul thus acknowledges his indebtedness to Philemon. He thereby prepares Philemon for the plea that he will make of him.

This thanksgiving, however, is somewhat problematic in the order or sequence of its ideas, as Lightfoot noted years ago:

> . . . all established principles of arrangement are defied [by Paul] in the anxiety to give expression to the thought which is uppermost for the moment. The clause *akouōn k.t.l.* [because I hear, etc.] is separated from *eucharistō k.t.l.* [I give thanks, etc.], on which it depends, by the intervening clause *mneian sou k.t.l.* [as I always remember, etc.], which introduces another thought. It itself interposes between two clauses, *mneian sou k.t.l.* and *hopōs hē koinōnia k.t.l.* [so the sharing, etc.], which stand in the closest logical and grammatical connexion with each other. Its own component elements are dislocated and inverted in the struggle of the several ideas for immediate utterance. And lastly, in *charan gar k.t.l.* [For . . . joy, etc.] there is again a recurrence to a topic which occurred in an earlier part of the sentence (*tē agapēn . . . eis pantas tous hagious* [love . . . God's dedicated people]) but which has been dropped, before it was exhausted, owing to the pressure of another more importunate thought. (*Colossians and Philemon*, 332)

Paul thanks God for Philemon's ability to refresh the hearts of Christians, subtly preparing him for the request that he will make of him in v 20 to refresh

Paul's heart too. "Paul prays neither for progress in his own faith as a consequence of his relation to Philemon nor for progress in Philemon's faith as a result of his fellowship with Paul" (Riesenfeld, "Faith and Love," 252–53).

NOTES

4. *I give thanks to my God.* Paul uses the verb *eucharistein,* as in 1 Thess 1:2; 1 Cor 1:4; Phil 1:3; cf. 2 Macc 1:11; Col 1:3; 2 Thess 1:3, where one also finds a thanksgiving following an epistolary greeting. See H. Patsch, *EDNT,* 2. 87–88. The phrase "my God" is also found in Phil 1:3; 4:19; 2 Cor 12:21; Rom 1:8. The sense of it is explained by what Paul says in the following words in this verse. Compare the same phrase in Pss 3:8; 5:3; 7:2, 4; 18:29; 22:2, where the LXX likewise has *ho theos mou.* Paul's prayer of thanksgiving to God is not uttered "through Jesus Christ," as it is in Rom 1:8. He prays to God because he knows that God graces such prayerful activity, and he calls upon God as an individual, prescinding from the mention of Timothy, the cosender of the letter.

as I always remember you in my prayers. The adverb *pantote,* "always," is placed between the two assertions in this verse, so that it could modify the preceding, "I give thanks to my God always" (as in Phil 1:3–4 [so C. F. D. Moule, *Colossians and Philemon,* 140; Vincent, *Word Studies,* 3. 516), or the following, "I always remember you in my prayers," as some commentators prefer (e.g. Stuhlmacher, *Brief an Philemon,* 32). The "you" is singular *(sou)* in the Greek text, referring directly to Philemon, even though the letter has been addressed to others as well. Thus Philemon is directly the object of Paul's prayer of thanksgiving and petition, and he remains the one addressed until v 22a. Paul makes use of the middle participle of *poiein* with an abstract noun as its object, thus employing an idiomatic construction *mneian poioumenos)* known since classical Greek times: Plato, *Phaedrus* 254A; *P. Lond.* 42.6; *TLNT,* 2. 496; BDF §310.1; MM, 414. Compare its use in 1 Thess 1:2; Rom 1:9; Eph 1:16.

5. *because I hear about the faith that you have in the Lord Jesus.* Or "I keep hearing," because the present participle may have an ongoing or iterative sense. So Paul states the reason or the basis for his prayer of thanksgiving: a kindly report about how Philemon has been living as a Christian, about his faith and love. Paul uses the participle *akouōn,* which is logically connected to the verb *eucharistō,* "I give thanks." He may be implying that Onesimus has reported all this to him about Philemon, or the information may have come from Epaphras. Paul does not specify the source of what he has heard. Compare 1 Thess 1:3; Col 1:3–4.

This verse is not uniformly transmitted in the various Greek MSS. MSS P^{61}, D, 323, 365, 629, 945, 1739 have the order *tēn pistin kai tēn agapēn, hēn echeis* . . . , "faith and love which you have . . . ," which makes faith precede the mention of love and which is what I am translating here. The difference in other MSS, which read *tēn agapēn kai tēn pistin,* "love and faith," may have resulted from a copyist's change imitating the order of Col 1:4 or Eph 1:15. In any case, the verse is not easy to translate, because it literally says "because I hear about the faith and love (*or:* the love and faith) that you have toward *(pros)* the Lord Jesus and toward *(eis)* all the saints." Two qualities of Philemon are mentioned, his "faith" and his "love," and two objects of them, "the Lord Jesus" and "all the saints." Because it is difficult to say what "all the saints" would mean as the object of "faith," I have divided up the compound assertion, so that "faith" is expressed "in the Lord Jesus" and "love" is shown "to all the saints." Paul is clearly lauding Philemon's virtues, his faith and his love, considering them as the sum of Christian conduct and the reason why he should be praying for Philemon. Carson prefers to understand *pistin* as "faithfulness" (*Colossians and Philemon,* 105), which would make Philemon's faithfulness and love have as objects both the Lord Jesus and the saints.

As in Rom 10:9 "the Lord Jesus" is recognized as the object of Philemon's faith, i.e. belief in the risen Christ (see *TLNT,* 2. 350), the basic belief of every Christian, which brings access to God's grace and His justification and salvation. For the combination *agapē eis,* cf. 1 Thess 3:12; 2 Cor 2:8; Rom 5:8; cf. Col 1:4; *IBNTG,* 68–69. For the combination *pistis pros,* cf. 4 Macc 15:24; 16:22; 1 Thess 1:8; *IBNTG,* 54. Some MSS (A, C. D*, 048) change *pros* to the more usual *eis.* MS D* adds *Christon.*

Some commentators (Theodore of Mopsuestia, Gnilka, Houlden, Jeremias, Lightfoot, Lohmeyer, Lohse, Moule, O'Brien, Stuhlmacher) call attention to a chiasm in the verse (a b b a): love, faith, for the Lord Jesus, for the saints. This view is perhaps correct, but it really depends on which MSS one is following, for various Greek MSS transmit the text differently, as noted above. Compare BDF §477.2; BDR §477.5.

and your love for all God's dedicated people. Lit. "for all the saints," i.e. fellow Christians. The substantivized adjective *hagioi,* "holy ones," is being used as a way of referring to those who have become Christians. The adjective *hagioi* likewise carries its OT nuance: persons or things dedicated to God and His cultic service (as in Lev 19:2; 11:44; Exod 19:5–6). Paul often refers to Christians as *hagioi* (e.g. Rom 1:7; 16:15; 1 Cor 1:2; 16:15; 2 Cor 1:1; 13:12; Phil 1:1; 1 Thess 3:13). Now he emphasizes "love" toward all of them, a virtue that suits the appeal he is making to Philemon (vv 7, 9, 16). It is a virtue that must flow from Christian faith (cf. Gal. 5:6).

6. *so that the sharing in your faith may be effective.* This purpose clause announces the generic content or object of Paul's petitionary prayer, with the conjunction *hopōs* (Schubert, *Form and Function,* 12). The prayer has to be understood as dependent on the second part of v 4, Paul's mention of his

constant remembrance of Philemon in prayer, because this verse otherwise lacks a main verb. Paul now prays that Philemon's faith may be always active and efficacious in its manifestation of love toward Christians who depend on him.

This verse is the most difficult one to understand in the whole letter. The first problem is the meaning of *koinōnia tēs pisteōs sou.*

(1) The noun *koinōnia* can denote "association, communion, close association" of two or more persons in some common interest, cause, or bonding (marital, societal, or communitarian), as in 1 Cor 1:9, "the association of His Son." Compare 2 Cor 13:13. This seems to be the second sense noted by Lightfoot (*Colossians and Philemon,* 333): "Your communion with God through faith."

(2) *Koinōnia* can also denote "participation, sharing" (in something [expressed as an objective genitive]), as in Wis 8:18; Phil 3:10; 2 Cor 8:14. Since the pronoun *sou* stands at the end of the phrase, the phrase might mean (a) "that your participation in the (Christian) faith may be(come) effective," with *sou* as a subjective genitive modifying the whole phrase. The sense would be that Philemon's sharing of Christian faith might come to be effective. So BAGD, 439; Chrysostom, Bengel, Bultmann (*TDNT* 1. 708), Collange, Dodd, Lohmeyer, Schlatter, Stuhlmacher (*Brief an Philemon,* 33, appealing to Phil 1:5), Winter. Or the phrase might mean (b) "that the participation (of others) in your faith may be(come) effective," with *sou* as a genitive of possession modifying only *pisteōs.* The sense would be that others (i.e. God's dedicated people, of v 5) may come to share in Philemon's Christian faith; for this Paul would be praying. This seems to be the way the RSV has understood the phrase; so too Campbell, Goodspeed, Moffatt, Weymouth, and as I prefer to take it. For if the meaning 2a were intended, one would expect *hē koinōnia sou tēs pisteōs,* as in Aristotle, *Politics* 3.1.13 §1276b; *koinonia politōn politeias,* "participation of citizens in government." See Campbell, *Three New Testament Studies,* 18.

(3) Sometimes *koinōnia* denotes concretely a "common donation, contribution," as in Rom 15:26. This does not seem to be the sense here, although Lightfoot (*Colossians and Philemon,* 333) considered this the more likely meaning: " 'Your friendly offices and sympathies, your kindly deeds of charity, which spring from your faith': comp. Phil i. 5." Apparently also Gnilka (*Philemonbrief,* 36).

(4) Some commentators understand *koinōnia* to mean "communication." So the Vg (*communicatio fidei tuae*); Vincent (*Philippians and Philemon,* 180): " 'The communication of thy faith' to others." That might be acceptable if it is merely another way of stating interpretation 2b above.

To my way of thinking, meaning 2b is to be preferred: Paul prays that God's dedicated people will share in the faith that marks Philemon's life and that it may produce results. In any case, *pistis* should not be restricted to the content sense of faith (*fides quae* of later theology), as Lohse has taken it (*Colossians and Philemon*, 193), but rather be understood in the sense of "faith" as a practice that has its effect in the way one lives (*fides qua* of later theology). See C. F. D. Moule, *Colossians and Philemon*, 142–43, for further explanation of these interpretations; Riesenfeld, "Faith and Love," 254–55.

effective. That is, may come to have results. The adjective *energēs*, however, is rendered in the Vg as *evidens* (evident, manifest), which seems to be a translation of Greek *enargēs* (evident), a reading that is not attested in any Greek MS of this letter. Jerome noted the difference: "evident" in Latin, but "effective" in Greek (*In Ep. ad Philemonem* [PL 26.646]). The Vg translates *koinōnia tēs pisteōs sou* as *communicatio fidei tuae evidens fiat*, giving to *koinōnia* a nuance of the "communication" of faith to other Christians (as does Vincent).

in the realization of all the good that is ours in Christ. Lit. "that is in us unto Christ." This phrase constitutes the second problem in the verse. Paul seems to see Philemon's effective faith promoting an understanding (*epignōsis*, "full knowledge," as in Phil 1:9) or a realization that comes to Christians about the "good" that is theirs because of their relation to Christ. Two things cause a problem in the understanding of the phrase: the meaning of *pantos agathou* and that of *eis Christon*.

(a) The best transmitted Greek text reads *en epignōsei pantos agathou tou en hēmin eis Christon* (translated in the lemma). MSS F and G, however, add *ergou* before *agathou*, "of every good deed"; MSS P[61], A, C, 048, 33, 629 omit the article after *agathou*; and MSS P[61], ℵ, F, G, P, 0278, 33, 1739, the Koine text-tradition, and ancient versions change *en hēmin*, "ours" (lit. "in us"), to *en hymin*, "yours" (lit. "in you" [plural]). Most of these changes do not provide a better understanding of the sentence; so it is better to stay with the text of N-A[27]. See *TCGNT*, 588, but compare Lohmeyer, *Brief an Philemon*, 176, who prefers the last-mentioned reading, as does Riesenfeld, who specifies the "good" as "the content of Christian hope," appealing to Eph 1:17–19; Heb 9:11; 10:1 *(ta mellonta agatha)*; Rom 8:28 and reading *tou en hymin*, "(all the good) that is yours" ("Faith and Love," 256). That, however, introduces a second plural form, which is questionable at this point in the letter, where the second singular otherwise predominates.

Paul seems to be speaking of an "understanding" that results from faith active in love (cf. Gal 5:6). Unfortunately, nothing specific is mentioned about what the "good" might be. On the "good" that faith in Christ can produce, see 1 Thess 5:15; Rom 15:2. The phrase *en hēmin* is not to be restricted to Paul, Timothy, and those mentioned in vv 23–24, *pace* Winter ("Paul's Letter," 4); it clearly refers to Christians in general who have put their faith in the risen Christ.

(b) Paul seems to be speaking of the good that flows from the realization promoted by effective faith in that it orients Christians properly "toward, unto Christ" *(eis Christon)*. The meaning of this last phrase is understood diversely. It refers to *pantos agathou* and formulates the goal of all the good that comes to Christians, (1) possibly "in view of Christ" (BAGD, 229 §4a or 4d; cf. 2 Cor 1:21; 11:3; Rom 16:5). Paul seems to be praying that through Philemon's faith a solidarity with others will be productive of a deeper knowledge for them of all the good that can come to "the saints" through their orientation unto Christ; or (2) perhaps in leading them to Christ as an eschatological goal (see 1 Cor 1:7; Phil 1:6; so Collange, *L'Epître*, 51; Lohmeyer, *Brief an Philemon*, 179; Stuhlmacher, *Brief an Philemon*, 33); or (3) possibly even "for the glory of Christ," as Lohse has understood it (*Colossians and Philemon*, 194; similarly Vincent, *Word Studies*, 3. 517). (4) Zerwick prefers to understand the phrase as "in the cause of Christ" (*GAGNT*, 2. 652), which tends to tone down the force of the preposition *eis*. (5) "To lead us into the fullness of Christian fellowship, that is, of Christ" (Wright, "*Christos* as 'Messiah,' " 55) is a tortuous, if not impossible, understanding of *Christos* in an incorporative sense, certainly in this letter, if not elsewhere in Paul's writings. Wright exaggerates when he tries to say that "the Messiahship of Jesus is explicitly significant for Paul"; apart from Rom 9:5, that is scarcely true. Nor does Paul "regularly" use *Christos* to connote or denote "the whole people of whom the Messiah is the representative" (ibid., 46).

Compare the LXX of Sir 17:7; Pss 36:27; 52:2 for parallels to the first five of the seven words in this verse; and 2 Cor 1:21; 11:3 for parallels to the prepositional phrase *eis Christon*. Compare 1QS 4:26, which also speaks of the "knowledge of good."

At the end of the verse some MSS (א^{2}, D, F, G, Ψ, 0278, 1739, 1881) add *Iēsoun*, which would mean "in Christ Jesus," a reading probably influenced by v 9.

7. *For I have experienced much joy and consolation in your love.* Lit. "I have much joy and consolation." So Paul expresses the motive of his prayer of thanks and petition for Philemon. He "rejoices with those who are rejoicing" (Rom 12:15), as Jerome recognized. Philemon's love has produced for Paul *charan pollēn kai paraklēsin*, "much joy and consolation," as he reflects on the specific advantage he has had in his imprisonment from the report about Philemon. He does not enter into detail about it, apart from what he will say in the rest of this sentence. *Pace* Winter ("Paul's Letter," 4), it hardly refers to "the comfort that Onesimus brought the community in prison." What "community" has been said to be in prison? Compare 2 Cor 7:4, 7, 13.

Paul uses an epistolary past tense, the aorist *eschon*, as in vv 12, 19, 21 below; cf. BDF §334; BDR §334. The past tense expresses the joy that he has as he writes, which will be in the past by the time his letter is read or is heard read by the addressees. MS D* reads *eschomen*, "we had," an inferior reading that upsets what Paul otherwise says in the first singular.

MSS of the Koine text-tradition read *charin*, "grace," instead of *charan*, "joy," which is the reading of MSS א, A, C, D, F, G. "Grace," however, would not make much sense here, as Gnilka notes (*Philemonbrief*, 37 n. 24), and "thankfulness," as in 1 Tim 1:12; 2 Tim 1:3, is not much better.

Origen, in his *Commentary on Matthew* 72 (GCS 38. 170) quotes v 7 of this letter to illustrate how Christians who visit the sick can have a good influence on other Christians.

because the hearts of God's dedicated people have been refreshed through you. Lit. "the inwards of the saints have been given rest through you." The term *splanchna* literally means "entrails, bowels, inwards," i.e. the viscera used figuratively as the seat of human emotion, especially sympathy or pity, as in the LXX of Sir 30:7; 33:5. It connotes an affective reaction directed toward other Christians in Colossae, but not necessarily "terror, grief, despondency," as Lightfoot would have it (*Colossians and Philemon*, 334). The term and its related verb *splanchnizesthai*, "be merciful," occur a few times in the LXX (e.g. 2 Macc 9:5–6; Prov 17:5), mostly in the late Greek writings, and only rarely in passages where they reflect a Hebrew term (either *reḥem*, "womb," or *beṭen*, "belly"). Compare Paul's use in 1 Cor 16:18; Phil 1:8. For C. F. D. Moule, both here and in vv 12, 20, it expresses the " 'inmost feelings,' 'very self'—that is, the recipient of the emotions rather than that which expresses them" (*Colossians and Philemon*, 144). "The word is . . . used for the whole person which in the depths of its emotional life has experienced refreshment through consolation and love" (H. Köster, *TDNT*, 7. 555; cf. O. Montevecchi, "Viscere," for a slightly different sense of the term). In v 20 Paul will ask Philemon to refresh his "heart" too. For parallels to such refreshment expressed by *anapauein*, see Matt. 11:28–29; 1 Cor 16:18; Ignatius, *Eph.* 2.1; *Smyrn.* 9.2; 10.1; cf. *TDNT*, 7. 548–59.

my brother. Paul repeats this term of Christian bonding here with emphasis, making it the last word at the end of his prayer. Compare v 20. See NOTE on v. 1, where the title is used of Timothy and, in MS D*, of Philemon.

BIBLIOGRAPHY

Boers, H., "*Agapē* and *Charis* in Paul's Thought," *CBQ* 59 (1997) 693–713.

Campbell, J. Y., "*Koinōnia* and Its Cognates in the New Testament," *JBL* 51 (1932) 352–80; repr. in his *Three New Testament Studies* (Leiden: Brill, 1965) 1–28.

Delaporte, L. J., "Fragment [copte] de l'épître à Philémon (5–8)," *RB* n.s. 2 (1905) 560–62.

George, A. R., *Communion with God in the New Testament* (London: Epworth, 1953) 183.

Jones, J. E., "The Letter to Philemon—an Illustration of Koinonia," *RevExp* 46 (1949) 454–66.

McDermott, M., "The Biblical Doctrine of *koinōnia*," *BZ* 19 (1975) 64–77, 219–33.

Montevecchi, O., "Viscere di misericordia," *RivB* 43 (1995) 125–33.

Mullins, T. Y., "The Thanksgivings of Philemon and Colossians," *NTS* 30 (1984) 288–93.

Pentecost, J. D., "Grace for the Sinner, Part II: An Exposition of Philemon 4–7," *BSac* 129 (1972) 218–25.

Riesenfeld, H., "Faith and Love Promoting Hope: An Interpretation of Philemon v. 6," *Paul and Paulinism: Essays in Honour of C. K. Barrett* (ed. M. D. Hooker and S. G. Wilson; London: SPCK, 1982) 251–57.

Seesemann, H., *Der Begriff* Koinōnia *im Neuen Testament* (BZNW 14; Giessen: Töpelmann, 1933) 79–83.

Wright, N. T., "*Christos* as 'Messiah' in Paul: Philemon 6," in his *The Climax of the Covenant: Christ and Law in Pauline Theology* (Edinburgh: Clark, 1991) 41–55.

III. The Body of the Letter (8–20)

[8]So, although I am emboldened enough in Christ to order you to do what is proper, [9]I would rather appeal out of love. I, Paul, am an elderly man and now a prisoner too for Christ Jesus. [10]I appeal to you on behalf of my child, Onesimus, whose father I have become in my imprisonment. [11]He was once useless to you, but now he has become quite useful [both] to you and to me. [12]I am sending him, that is, my very own heart, back to you. [13]I would have preferred to keep him here with me, so that he might serve me on your behalf during my imprisonment for the gospel; [14]but I did not want to do anything without your consent, so that the good you do might not be forced but come of your own free will. [15]For perhaps he has been separated for a while for this very reason, that you may have him back for ever, [16]no longer as a slave but as more than a slave, as a beloved brother. He is such to me, but how much more to you, both as a human being and in the Lord. [17]If, then, you consider me your partner, welcome him as you would welcome me. [18]If he has wronged you in any matter or owes you anything, charge that to me. [19]I, Paul, write this with my own hand; I will repay it—not to mention that you owe me even your own self. [20]Yes, my brother, may I profit from you in the Lord. Refresh my heart in Christ!

COMMENT

In contrast to the prescript of this letter, which mentions three individuals and the house-church that meets at Philemon's dwelling, the body of the letter addresses only Philemon in the singular. It appeals to Philemon's goodwill to welcome back Onesimus. It likewise acknowledges how useful Onesimus has been to him, indirectly suggesting that Philemon might not only forgive Onesimus but also release him so that he might return to work with Paul in his evangelization. What Paul now says is basically a form of intercession for Onesimus, a form that is otherwise known from contemporary literature in the Greco-Roman world. The letter thus deals with a household matter, not a matter of major church concern, despite the greetings to multiple persons and the house-church of the prescript, *pace* S. B. C. Winter.

In order to appreciate the delicacy of Paul's argument, it is worth comparing this letter with one of Pliny the Younger (A.D. 61–112), who wrote in Latin a similar letter of intercession on behalf of a *libertus* who had strayed in the service of his patron, Sabinianus (quoted in the Introduction §32). It reveals how Paul's letter fits into the contemporary Greco-Roman setting. Whereas Pliny pleads for a *libertus*, "freedman," with the master who is his *patronus*, "patron," Paul pleads for one who is still *doulos*, "a slave," in Philemon's household. In contrast to the way Pliny interceded with Sabinianus for a *libertus* who had done him harm and damage, Paul does not plead with Philemon to exercise Stoic clemency; he calls rather on Philemon's faith and love as a Christian.

In vv 8–10 Paul describes his own situation as a prisoner and an elderly man and makes nothing of his status as an apostle. Before he even mentions the slave's name, Paul sets forth his relationship to him, who has been converted to Christianity through Paul's instrumentality. In vv 11–12 Paul plays on the meaning of Onesimus' name, emphasizing how "useful" he has become to him and treating Onesimus as if he were part of himself, his very own "heart." In vv 13–14 Paul acknowledges that, though he would have preferred to keep Onesimus with him, he recognizes Philemon's legal right to the slave; and so he will not deprive Philemon of the good that Onesimus can still do for him. Although Paul states his desire to have Onesimus to work with him as an assistant, he is still sending Onesimus back to Philemon "for ever" (*hina aiōnion auton apechēs*). This complicates the understanding of Paul's intention in writing. In any case, Paul stresses that he is sending Onesimus back as "more than a slave, as a beloved brother," i.e. a fellow Christian (vv 15–16). Finally, in vv 17–20 Paul begs Philemon to welcome Onesimus as he would welcome Paul himself, assuring Philemon that he will account for any damages he has suffered because of Onesimus.

Thus Paul writes as the skilled advocate, as Gnilka rightly recognizes (*Philemonbrief*, 53). Paul presents his case with much personal reflection and subtly seeks to get from Philemon a good welcome for Onesimus. The meaning of the slave's name is exploited in Paul's argument, and emphasis is put on his Christian status.

NOTES

8. *So*. Paul uses the traditional conjunction *dio*, "wherefore, accordingly, so it is that," to link the body of his letter immediately to the thanksgiving and petition; see BDF §451.5. The Vg translates it as *propter quod*, so that the antecedent of *quod* must be all that for which Paul prayed in vv 4–7. Lightfoot paraphrased the transition thus: "Encouraged by these tidings of thy loving spirit, I prefer to entreat, where I might command" (*Colossians and Philemon*, 335). Compare J. T. Sanders, "The Transition from Opening Epistolary Thanksgiving to Body in the Letters of the Pauline Corpus," *JBL* 81 (1962) 348–62, esp. 355.

although I am emboldened enough in Christ to order you to do what is proper. Lit. "having much boldness in Christ to order you (to do) what is required." The participle *echōn*, "having," has to be understood in a concessive sense (BDF §418.3; *IBNTG*, 102). Although Paul recognizes the good qualities of Philemon and that his Christian relationship with him is excellent so that, given his God-given authority as an apostle (1 Cor 9:1; Rom 11:13; Gal 1:12), he might easily make use of his apostolic *exousia*, "right" (2 Cor 10:8), to speak plainly and demand obedience from Philemon, he appeals rather to his love and goodwill. So Paul expresses the ground or basis for his plea. *Parrhēsia*, "frankness, openness, boldness," seems to mean here freedom to speak peremptorily or with authority (*TDNT*, 5. 883), and without fear (cf. 2 Cor 3:12). As Caird notes, Paul is not saying "that it takes courage or effrontery to speak with authority to his friend, but that as an apostle he has the right to do so, a right he does not propose to invoke" (*Paul's Letters*, 221). Perhaps Paul means that Philemon should think twice about declining Paul's request. See further S. B. Marrow, *Speaking the Word Fearlessly*, 31.

Paul finds that this *parrhēsia* comes to him "in Christ," because he is aware that his call as an apostle has come from "a revelation of Jesus Christ" (Gal 1:12). In light of that call Paul feels that he has an apostolic right to give instructions. Paul even speaks of ordering Philemon, employing *epitassein*, a strong verb that he does not otherwise use (*TDNT*, 8. 37), and thus he forgoes that right in this case.

The term *to anēkon* expresses what is "proper, fitting, suitable" in a given set of circumstances, often that which is legally obligatory (Schlier, *TDNT*, 1. 360). The idea was used often in contemporary Hellenistic philosophy, especially that of the Stoics, to express what was expected of citizens, husbands, fathers (see Martin, *NIDNTT*, 3. 930); but the verb occurs only a few times in the NT (cf. Col 3:18; Eph 5:4) and in Greek literature as a whole. "What is proper" is not what Philemon would be expected to do according to the law, which might permit the punishment of Onesimus, but rather what is fitting and appropriate for Philemon as a Christian, and that is explained in vv 10–13.

9. *I would rather appeal out of love*. Lit. "I rather appeal because of love." Paul says this, realizing that Christian faith must "work itself out in love" (Gal 5:6), i.e. love in the general Christian sense of fraternal affection, and not Paul's specific love for Philemon, or even Philemon's love mentioned in v 7. Such love involves a freedom from self-regard or selfishness and an outgoing affection for others (Phil 2:4); it characterizes the kind of faith by which a Christian must live. So Paul avoids trying to elicit obedience by an order. Note too that Pliny in his plea for the *libertus* of Sabinianus also argued out of love: *Amasti hominem et, spero, amabis* (You once had affection for [this] human being, and, I hope, you will have it again; see Introduction §32).

The verb *parakalein* is used now in the sense of entreaty or petition (as in

2 Cor 2:8; 12:8), and not of exhortation or encouragement, as in most Pauline passages. Compare O. Schmitz, *TDNT*, 5.793–94; C. J. Bjerkelund, *Parakalô*, 119–20; Mullins, "Petition," 48–49. Compare what Ignatius of Antioch writes in *Eph.* 3:1–2, where a similar argument is employed: not a command, but love.

I, Paul, am an elderly man. Lit. "being such a one as Paul, an elderly man," i.e. being such as one knows me to be. The participle *ōn*, "being," could be taken either as concessive ("although I am") or causal ("because I am," cf. *IBNTG*, 102). Paul identifies himself by name and thus implies his authority, given his seniority, in virtue of which he pleads with the younger Philemon. This part of the verse describes his current status, an elderly man and a prisoner, and thus offers a basis for the plea he is making. For respect due to a hoary head, see Lev 19:32; Sir 8:6.

All Greek MSS read *presbytēs*, "an elderly man," i.e. someone between fifty and fifty-six years of age, as advanced age was reckoned in those days. The physician Hippocrates (actually Pseudo-Hippocrates), in *Peri Hebdomadōn*, quoted by Philo (*De opificio mundi* 36 §105), lists the seven stages of human life as *paidion, pais, meirakion, neaniskos, anēr, presbytēs, gerōn*, "little boy, boy, lad, young man, man, elderly man, old man." Philo explains these stages as multiples of seven years: *neaniskos* denotes someone aged twenty-one to twenty-eight, *anēr* someone up to forty-nine, and *presbytēs* someone aged fifty to fifty-six. However, one finds *presbytēs* used of persons still older in Greek papyri (cf. *P. Lond.* 50, 62, 95; MM, 535); and Hippocrates (*Aphorismi* 3.30–31) lists *presbytēs* as the final stage of human life. Compare F. Boll, "Die Lebensalter," *Neue Jahrbücher für das klassische Altertum* 31 (1913) 89–154, esp. 114–18; E. Eyben, "Die Einteilung des menschlichen Lebens im römischen Altertum," *Rheinisches Museum* 116 (1973) 150–90. *Presbytēs* in the sense of "elderly man" is also found in Luke 1:18; Titus 2:2; *Mart. Pol.* 7.2–3; Josephus, *J.W.* 1.16.4 §312. The Latin translation of Origen's *Commentary on Matthew* 66 (GCS 38. 157) rendered *presbytēs* as *senex*, as did Jerome (*In Ep. ad Philemonem* 9 [PL 26. 647]).

Some commentators (Benson, E. Haupt), however, prefer to adopt the conjecture of R. Bentley (*Bentleii Critica Sacra* [ed. A. A. Ellis; Cambridge: Deighton, Bell & Co., 1862] 73), who proposed to add an *epsilon* and read *presbeutēs*, thus making Paul "an ambassador" of Christ (comparing the verb *presbeuein* in 2 Cor 5:20; Eph 6:20). Bentley suggested this because in Acts 7:58 Saul/Paul is said to have been *neanias* at the stoning of Stephen; so he considered that Paul could not now be calling himself "an elderly man." He was apparently unaware of Hippocrates' stages and Philo's explanation of them, preferring to read: *hōs palai presbeutēs nyn de kai desmios*, "as once an ambassador, but now a prisoner too." That produces an interesting contrast, but it is nevertheless problematic, above all because Paul does not otherwise use the noun *presbeutēs*.

Still others (Theophylact, Calvin, Bjerkelund, Caird, Carson, Goodspeed, Gülzow, Hort, Houlden, Lightfoot, Lohmeyer, Martin, C. F. D. Moule, Ogg, Petersen, Preiss, Soards, Suhl, Wickert), as well as some versions (RSV, NEB, REB), maintain that *presbytēs* itself can mean "ambassador." They claim that the two Greek forms were interchanged in the sense of "ambassador" by scribes of the LXX in such passages as 2 Chr 32:31; 1 Macc 13:21; 14:21, 22; 15:17; 2 Macc 11:34 and that they were indifferently used with this meaning. Compare also Polyaenus, *Strategemata* 8.9.1; *TCGNT*, 588.

Pace C. F. D. Moule (*Colossians and Philemon*, 144), the meaning "ambassador" does not "make excellent sense" in this context, despite the contrast that it makes with *desmios*, "prisoner." It is rather unlikely, as Bornkamm rightly recognized (*TDNT*, 6. 683), because Paul "hesitates to make express assertion of his apostolic authority." It has been judged similarly by T. Zahn (*Introduction to the New Testament* [3 vols.; Grand Rapids, Mich.: Kregel, 1953], 1. 457 n. 6), Vincent, von Soden, Meinertz, Dibelius (*An Philemon*, 104): it turns Paul's line of thought upside down. More recent English versions (NAB, NIV, NJB, NRSV) avoid that meaning. See especially J. N. Birdsall, "*Presbytēs* in Philemon 9," who shows in detail that Bentley's conjecture is "totally unfeasible"; it should be deleted from the *apparatus criticus* of N-A^{27}.

The VL, the Vg, and some Latin authors (Pelagius, Ambrosiaster) understood the words *toioutos ōn hōs Paulos* as referring to Philemon, *cum sis talis ut Paulus senex*, i.e. "since you are such (a person) as Paul, an elderly man." This would make Philemon as old as Paul, and Ambrosiaster so interpreted it: *coaevum aetate* (*Ad Filemonem* 1.9 [CSEL 81/3. 339]); similarly Pelagius (*In Ep. ad Philemonem* [PLSup 1. 1374]).

now a prisoner too for Christ Jesus. Paul writes not only as an "elderly man" but also as a "prisoner for Christ Jesus," another reason why his plea should be heard. Paul repeats the description of himself that he used in v 1 above (see NOTE there), now as a title of respect, to which he adds "for Christ Jesus," i.e. on account of Christ Jesus (see *IBNTG*, 113). Paul shares the weakness and the humiliation of Christ, as Lohse notes (*Colossians and Philemon*, 199), but he is also one who suffers hardships and deserves consideration because of the honorable cause to which he is devoted and for which he suffers (Phil 1:12–13). Compare Eph 4:1.

10. *I appeal to you on behalf of my child, Onesimus.* This verse formulates Paul's plea, as he again entreats Philemon, repeating the substance of v 9. Paul delays the naming of Onesimus to this verse, and indeed to the very end of the sentence, so that he names him only after he has shown that the slave is now a Christian; thus he renders Philemon more favorably disposed to his "child." Philemon has probably heard little about Onesimus since he departed, until he reads this sentence.

Paul uses *parakalein* with the preposition *peri* and the genitive of the person concerned in the sense of "on behalf of," as in *P. Oxy.* 7. 1070.8; cf. 10. 1298.4; 12. 1494.6; W. Dittenberger, *Sylloge inscriptionum graecarum* (4 vols.; Hildesheim: Olms, 1960), 3. 1170:3; Appian, *Punic Wars* 136. *Pace* Knox and Winter ("Paul's Letter," 6), *parakalō se peri tou emou teknou* does not mean " 'I ask you *for* my child' (Onesimus is the object of the request)." Winter says that "scholars disagree on the meaning of the preposition *peri*" but gives no evidence of the disagreement and cites no one who would support her interpretation, apart from Knox (*Philemon among the Letters*, 16, 22–23), whom she is following. Compare Bjerkelund, *Parakalô*, 120–21; Nordling, "Onesimus Fugitivus," 110–13; Stuhlmacher, *Brief an Philemon*, 38: "bedeutet nach dem Fortgang unseres Briefes 'bitten für' und nicht, wie Knox möchte, 'bitten um.' "

Paul calls Onesimus *to emon teknon*, "my child," thus acknowledging a relationship between the slave and himself, which has not previously existed. *Teknon* expresses here not a physical but a symbolic relationship, as in 1 Cor 4:14–15, 17. The conversion of Onesimus was God's work, but God often works through human agents; in this case, through Paul, who regards himself as a father in Christ to Onesimus; cf. Gal 4:19. Carson contrasts Paul, the onetime Pharisee and heir of Jewish exclusiveness and remoteness, with the Gentile slave, "from the very dregs of Roman society" (*Colossians and Philemon*, 108), with whom Paul now associates himself, in order to bring out the meaning of "my child."

Nomen est omen (the name is an omen), and Paul is playing on the meaning of *Onēsimos* and its relation to *achrēston* later in the verse. The name *Onēsimos* means "useful, profitable one," and it was in current use at the time Paul writes. A. L. Connolly has listed about sixty instances of its use in various inscriptions, a third of which come from Ephesus, and many others from Asia Minor (*NDIEC* 4 [1987] 179–81). It was often used for slaves (e.g. Menander, *Epitrepontes* 2a; Galen, *De optima doctrina* 1.82; *P. Cair. Zen.* 2 [1926] 59148 and 59285; cf. Lightfoot, *Colossians and Philemon*, 308–9) and thus described their worth to their owners or masters. It was, however, a name often borne also by many freemen. As a name of a slave, it was similar to others: *Karpos* (= fruit[ful]), *Chrēsimos* (= useful), *Chrēstos* (= good, profitable), *Onēsiphoros* (= bringing profit), *Symphoros* (= suitable, profitable). For examples of Latin *Onesimus* as a slave name, see *CIL*, 3. 323 §2146; 3. 359 §2723; 3. 986 §6107.

whose father I have become in my imprisonment. Lit. "whom I have begotten in chains," or "in my chains," if one follows the reading *en tois desmois mou* of MSS $\aleph^2$, C, D^1, Ψ, 0278, 1739. Paul has begotten Onesimus, because Onesimus has been converted to Christian faith through his instrumentality. Being a child begotten by the imprisoned Paul, the Christian Onesimus is especially dear to Paul.

For instances of Paul referring to himself as "father" to other Christian converts, see 1 Cor 4:14–15, 17; Gal 4:19; cf. 1 Pet 1:3. The same image is found in Essene texts (1QH 7:20–21: the Teacher of Righteousness says in a hymn to God, "You have made me a father for the children of kindness"; cf. CD 13:9). In later rabbinic literature, a teacher who instructs others in *Tôrāh* is called a father (*b. Sanhedrin* 19b; cf. Str-B, 3. 339), and a convert to Judaism is compared to a "child just born" (*b. Yebamot* 22a). Compare 2 Kgs 2:12; Philo, *Leg. ad Gaium* 8 §58).

Another possible translation would be "whom I have begotten as Onesimus." It would, then, play even more so on the meaning of the slave's name, but it would not necessarily mean that "Onesimus" was the Christian name given to the new convert, as Knox would have it (*Philemon among the Letters*, 24–25). As R. P. Martin has said, "It is just as likely that he became true to his slave name at this time" (*Colossians and Philemon*, 164).

The form *Onēsimon* is accusative, which means that it does not stand in apposition to genitive *teknou*, "child." It is found in the Greek text after the masculine accusative relative pronoun, and perhaps that is why it is accusative, attracted to the pronoun *hon*, the object of the verb *egennēsa*, "I have begotten" (Lightfoot compares Mark 6:16: *hon egō apekephalisa Iōannēn*). After the pronoun *hon*, some MSS (A, 69) and the Syriac Harclean version add *egō*, which merely emphasizes the subject of the verb *egennēsa*, but its absence in other MSS may be owing to haplography (from egō egen*nēsa*).

Paul describes his imprisonment metaphorically as *en tois desmois*, "in chains," but his arrest was probably of the sort called *custodia libera* (liberal detention) in the Roman world of his time, or *phylakē adesmos* in the Greek world. It denoted, however, a form of detention that would prevent escape (see Rapske, *The Book of Acts and Paul in Roman Custody*, 28, 206–9).

11. *He was once useless to you.* Paul now plays formally on the name of the slave, using the adjectives *achrēstos*, "useless," and *euchrēstos*, "quite useful," in the second part of the verse. The first means just the opposite of *Onēsimos*, denoting someone who is *an-onētos*, "useless." The Apostle gives no details about how Onesimus became "useless" to Philemon, but he is clearly playing on the meaning of the slave's name. Onesimus became "useless" either by running away or, more likely, as v 18 implies, by having stolen something from Philemon or caused him some financial damage or loss. It was something that aggravated his relationship to his master. In any case, Onesimus has become like the proverbially useless Phrygian slave (Cicero quotes the proverb *Phrygem plagis fieri solere meliorem* [A Phrygian usually becomes better because of a whipping] in *Pro Flacco* 65). For other instances of puns on names, see Aeschylus, *Agamemnon* 671; *Prometheus Bound* 85–86; Sophocles, *Ajax* 430–31.

but now he has become quite useful [both] to you and to me. Paul insists that Onesimus is now living up to his name, having become a different person, a changed man. Onesimus' past has been, as it were, canceled, for he now belongs to Christ and is a new man in Christ through faith and baptism. Paul also contrasts what was with what now is, as elsewhere in his writings (Rom 3:21; cf. Col 1:21–22). Paul recognizes the legal priority of Onesimus' relationship to Philemon, even though he willingly admits how "useful" Onesimus has become to him, ever since the slave has become a Christian. The phrase "and to me" sounds like an afterthought, because the order *soi kai emoi* is unusual in Greek, where custom dictated that the first personal pronoun precede the second or third. So Onesimus has outlived the proverbial role of the "Phrygian slave." MSS ℵ[2], A, C, D, 0278, 1739, 1881 omit *kai*, "both."

Paul uses the compound adjective *euchrēstos*, lit. "really useful, of great value," a compound of the adverb *eu*, "well," and the adjective *chrēstos*, "profitable, useful," and thus the opposite of *achrēstos* (see MM, 268). Compare 2 Tim 2:21; 4:11; Plato, *Republic* 3.18 §411B (*chrēsimon ex achrēstou . . . epoiēsen*, "made [him/it?] useful instead of useless"); Shepherd of Hermas, *Vis.* 3.6.7; *Mand.* 5.1.6.

Some commentators (Justin Martyr, *Apol.* 1.4.1; Dunn, Lohmeyer, Lohse, Stuhlmacher) think that Paul, in using *achrēstos*, is playing on the name *Christos*, because in Roman times *a-chrēstos* would have been pronounced by itacism as *a-christos*, and so the adjective might have meant something like "non-Christian." That, however, is far-fetched, because "non-Christian" would have been *a-christianos* (see Acts 11:26). See further Lightfoot, *Colossians and Philemon*, 338; Gnilka, *Philemonbrief*, 46.

12. *I am sending him, that is, my very own heart, back to you.* Lit. "whom I am sending back to you, him, that is my very own inwards." So the Apostle describes his newfound relationship to Onesimus and calls attention to his fulfillment of the legal requirements. Paul sees Christian Onesimus as part of himself (see *TLNT*, 3. 275); on *splanchna*, translated as "heart," see NOTE on v 7, and note its occurrence again in v 20. "It is as if Paul, in the runaway slave, came to Philemon in person with his claim to experience love. Then frequent use of the word [*splanchna*] in this short letter shows how personally Paul was involved in the matter" (H. Koester, *TDNT*, 7. 555). Lightfoot compares the sense of this word here with Artemidorus, *Oneir.* 1.44: *hoi paides splanchna legontai*, "the children are said to be inwards." The same term is used to identify the self of the writer in Eusebius, *Historia ecclesiastica* 7.21.3; cf. Gregory Nazianzen, *Oratio* 3.7 (SC 247. 250).

The verb *anepempsa* is again an epistolary aorist; see NOTE on v 7 and cf. Col 4:7–9; *IBNTG*, 12. The basic meaning of *anapempein* is "send up," e.g. in the sense of sending up (to a higher authority), as in Luke 23:7; Acts 25:21, although it is employed at times as the equivalent of the simple verb *pempein*, "send" (Josephus, *J.W.* 1.18.4 §358; 2.21.3 §605; *Ant.* 18.9.1 §313). It is often used, however, in the sense of "sending back," as in Luke 23:11, 15; Josephus, *J.W.* 1.33.8 §666; *Ant.* 3.4.1. §72; *1 Clem.* 65:1; Plutarch, *Solon* 4.3 §80; Pindar,

Isthmian Odes 7.10; Origen, *Comm. in Joan.* 28.6.43 (GCS 4. 395). To use the first meaning here, as Knox and Winter do, is strange, because Paul is not referring Onesimus' case "to a higher court" (*Philemon among the Letters*, 25) or to a "proper higher authority" (Winter, "Paul's Letter," 7). Paul is referring Onesimus' case to his legal owner or to his master for a decision. But one cannot gloss over the problem of how Onesimus came to be with Paul or the meaning of the next phrase, despite C. F. D. Moule's temptation to go along with Knox's understanding of this verb (*Colossians and Philemon*, 145). Moreover Knox's interpretation of Luke 23:11, 15 is simply wrong; in those Lucan instances the verb means "send back." Paul is using the verb in the second sense, for he is sending Onesimus back to Philemon; see BAGD, 59; *EDNT*, 1. 87; Nordling, "Onesimus Fugitivus," 108; *TLNT*, 1. 107–10, esp. 108. Compare Deut 23:16–17 (15–16E), where the Mosaic law said that one was not to return a runaway slave to his master (on which see Introduction §48).

In sending Onesimus back to Philemon, Paul was taking a risk, as was Onesimus too. Neither of them knew how Philemon, the master, would react to the return of Onesimus, or whether Philemon would be convinced by Paul's letter, which the slave was carrying. Onesimus was probably willing to take this risk in order to show that he was indeed *euchrēstos*, as Paul was saying.

The construction, however, is strange, because it is a Greek relative clause, introduced by the pronoun *hon*, "whom," which is then resumed by *auton*, lit. "him," meant to intensify the relative pronoun itself. This has been explained as a Semitism, imitating the indeclinable Hebrew *'ăšer* or Aramaic *dî*, which, being indeclinable, normally has to have such a resumptive pronoun to explain it (see BDF §197). Such an explanation seems strange for a letter like this. It may be rather a slip that is not otherwise unknown in the Greek language, even in the classical period (ibid.). In this case, the *auton* has been added because of the following explanatory clause that stands in apposition to it.

On the texual transmission of this verse and its unimportant variant readings, see Lohse, *Colossians and Philemon*, 201 n. 40, and *TCGNT*, 589. The text used in N-A^{27} is based on MSS א*, A, 33, to which copyists have often added *proslabou*, "welcome," from v 17.

13. *I would have preferred to keep him here with me, so that he might serve me on your behalf during my imprisonment for the gospel.* Or, "in your stead," because the sense of the phrase *hyper sou* is not unambiguous; see *IBNTG*, 64; ZBG §91; H. Riesenfeld, *TDNT*, 8. 513. It is not clear just what it would mean in either sense, except that Paul implies that Philemon himself would have wanted to assist Paul directly. Dunn (*Colossians and Philemon*, 306) rightly states that what is said here indicates that Onesimus himself was anxious to return to Colossae and Philemon's house. Paul makes use of *katechein* in the sense of "retain, keep, hold on to," as in the LXX of Gen 24:56; Philo, *Legum allegoria* 3.70 §197 (cf. *TLNT*, 2. 286). Underlying Paul's implied request is

the conviction that he expresses in Gal 6:6: "Let the one who is taught the Word share all good things with him who teaches." This could be applied not only to Philemon but also to Onesimus, Paul's most recent convert who has been taught the Word.

Paul gives a vague reason for his own imprisonment, *diakonia tou euangeliou.* This could mean either "ministry of evangelization" or "service of the gospel," because it is hard to say whether Paul is using *euangelion* in the content sense, "the gospel" that he preaches (as in 1 Thess 3:2; Gal 1:7; Phil 1:27; Rom 1:9), or in the active sense, "evangelization" (as in Gal 2:7; Phil 4:3, 15; 1 Cor 9:14b, 18b). Both senses are found in his writings; see *PAHT*, 38 (§PT31); *TLNT*, 2. 89.

In the Greek text the verse begins with a relative connective *hon*, which is the object of the verb *eboulomēn . . . katechein* (see BDF §458). The verb *eboulomēn* might again be an epistolary imperfect, but it seems rather to have a conditional sense, expressing the forgoing of an attainable wish (without *an;* BDF §359.2; ZBG §356; cf. Mayser, *Grammatik*, 2/1. 227 and *IBNTG*, 9). Caird sees a difference in the past tenses used here, taking the imperfect *eboulomēn* in v 13 as meaning "I had it in mind," whereas the aorist *ethelēsa* in v 14 would mean "I decided not to (do anything)" (*Paul's Letters*, 222; cf. Lightfoot, *Colossians and Philemon*, 339). Compare the similar request in Ignatius, *Eph.* 2.1 (see Knox, *Philemon among the Letters*, 99–100).

14. *but I did not want to do anything without your consent.* Paul acknowledges the master's legal right to the slave, but hints that he would like to have Onesimus back to work with him. Onesimus may have repented, but he still has to make restitution. Thus Paul gives up Onesimus, but a greater sacrifice is demanded of Onesimus. What Paul says here does not negate the wish that he expressed indirectly in v 13; it remains even though he now acknowledges Philemon's prior concern.

The noun *gnōmē*, lit. "purpose, intention," or "opinion," is often used in a technical, legal sense of "previous knowledge" or "consent" in some papyrus texts (see MM, 129; BAGD, 163) and in 2 Macc 4:39; Josephus, *Ant.* 7.2.2 §60; 18.9.4 §336; Ignatius of Antioch, *Pol.* 4.1; 5.2. It is not clear here whether Paul uses the word "consent" in the legal sense or merely in a general way expressing his interest in fair play (see Bultmann, *TDNT*, 1. 717). For a parallel to *chōris tēs sēs gnōmēs*, see Polybius, *Hist.* 2.21.4.

so that the good you do might not be forced. Lit. "so that your good might not be as from constraint," i.e. not even have the semblance of constraint. Again, Paul rhetorically hints at the authority that he could have used in Onesimus' case. Rather, Philemon's reception of Onesimus must be kindly and not even *seem* to be forced. Compare 2 Cor 9:7 and the letter of Pliny the Younger to Sabinianus, *Ep.* 9.21: *Vereor, ne videar non rogare sed cogere* (I fear that . . . I may seem rather to compel than to request). On the use of *to agathon*, a substantivized adjective with an article, see BDF §263.1. It is hard to say just what that "good" might be, since Paul has left it unspecified. It would seem to mean that Philemon's kindly reception of Onesimus is a minimum, but other aspects might also be possible.

but come of your own free will. Paul's phrase *kata hekousion* resembles the LXX expression used for a "freewill offering" (Num 15:3). This phrase stresses that Paul is in the long run completely dependent on Philemon's willingness to go along with what Paul is requesting, and it stresses the tact that Paul is employing. Compare 2 Cor 9:7; 1 Pet 5:2.

Paul touches here on a delicate human problem: that the good that humans do must come from them spontaneously and of their own free will, and not because of any necessity or constraint. That is the essence of being human. In his *Homilies on Jeremiah*, Origen cites this verse to show how even God rules and seeks to get human subjects to do what is right not by force but by their own goodwill (20.2 [SC 238. 256]; see J. C. Smith, *Origen: Homilies on Jeremiah* (FC; Washington, D.C.: Catholic University of America, 1998] 224). Compare Origen, *De oratione* 29.15 [GCS 3. 390–91]; J. J. O'Meara, *Origen: Prayer* (ACW 19; Westminster, Md.: Newman; London: Longmans, Green, 1954) 124.

15. *For perhaps.* The conjunction *gar* introduces an added reason that prompts Paul's decision and his plea for Onesimus. The adverb *tacha* creates something of a problem for commentators, in view of what has been said in v 14. C. F. D. Moule claims that it "makes it difficult to interpret the present verse otherwise than as a reference to the possibility of its *not* being his master's intention (*gnōmē*) to part with Onesimus" (*Colossians and Philemon*, 146–47), whereas Gnilka thinks that Moule has thus set the matter upside down (*Philemonbrief*, 51 n. 72). Compare BDF §102.2. Actually the adverb introduces a cautious added thought.

he has been separated for a while. Lit. "for this was he separated for an hour," i.e. for a short time (as in 2 Cor 7:8; Gal 2:5). Paul does not say that Onesimus has fled but uses a more euphemistic verb, meaning only that Onesimus has been parted from the household in which he normally served. The Greek text does not state from whom Onesimus has been separated, but the Vg adds *a te*, "from you," as do many modern versions (e.g. NAB, NIV, NRSV, RSV) and commentators (e.g. Lohse, Stuhlmacher); some employ a paraphrase that means the same thing (e.g. REB, NJB).

Gnilka rightly has preserved the more literal translation (*Philemonbrief*, 39, 50), because Paul clearly does not want Philemon to be reminded of the damage he has suffered. Moreover the verb *echōristhē* has to be understood as a theological passive, i.e. "separated" by God (see ZBG §236), even connoting God's hidden purpose (Lohse, *Colossians and Philemon*, 202). Onesimus' absence may have been bad for Philemon, but it has been turned into an act of divine providence for him, which Paul would not want to thwart. Hence he emphasizes that Onesimus has been separated from Philemon so that Philemon can have him back for ever as a Christian and brother. Compare Gen 45:5: "God sent me here before you to preserve life," clarifies Joseph to his brothers in Egypt, as he reveals himself to them and in effect excuses what they had done to him. And again, "You plotted evil against me, but God has planned it for good, to achieve what is now being done . . ." (Gen 50:20). Compare Jerome, *In Ep. ad Philemonem* 15 (PL 26. 649).

for this very reason. The preposition *dia* is used with the accusative to express cause (ZBG §112). Similarly in Rom 1:26; 3:25; 4:16, 25; 5:12; 11:28; 13:6; 1 Cor 4:17; cf. Col 1:9; 1 Tim 1:16.

that you may have him back for ever. Lit. "have him back (as) eternal," i.e. permanently. The phrase *doulon aiōnion,* "slave for ever," is found in the LXX of Job 40:28 (= Hebrew *ʿebed ʿôlām* [English 41:4]). Paul's use of the adjective *aiōnion* carries the same nuance as the prepositional phrase *eis ton aiōna* in Exod 21:6; Lev 25:46; Deut 15:17, which speak similarly of a slave's service "for ever." The adjective *aiōnion* stands in contrast to the temporal phrase *pros hōran,* "for an hour/time," of the preceding clause. Onesimus and Philemon have been separated "for a while," but the new relationship will continue "for ever." The sense of the adjective *aiōnion,* however, may be double: the providential separation of Onesimus from Philemon "for a while" may mean that the slave is now returning more faithful for lifelong service; but Paul may also be alluding to the new relationship existing between them: Paul, Philemon, and Onesimus are now Christians, related in an eternal sense that not even death can undo. Clearly, Onesimus does not return as the same person who departed from Philemon's house.

The verb *apechein* may mean either "to have back, to have in return" (restitution) or "to have to the full" (completion), a bookkeeping nuance, as in Phil 4:18. The former is the preferred sense (because of vv 13–14), especially since Paul is sending Onesimus back to Philemon. Knox preferred to understand the verb as "have or receive in full," translating it as "possess": "in order that he might thenceforth possess him *not as a slave,* but in a quite new sense, *forever.* Onesimus has now become his brother in Christ" (*Philemon among the Letters,* 26–27). For Spicq, however, it denotes "will recover him . . . for good in heaven as a brother for eternity" (*TLNT,* 1. 165). Compare Basil the Great, *Detailed Rules* 11 (PG 31. 948A).

Verses 15–16 are quoted in a fragment of Ignatius, *Pol.* (lines 15–17), in a paragraph that has to be added to *Pol.* 4.3. It reads *epechēs* instead of *apechēs.* The verb *epechein* is only a strengthened form of *echein,* "have" (see MM, 232); it does not change much the sense of Phlm 16. See J. H. Crehan, "A New Fragment," 24.

16. *no longer as a slave but as more than a slave, as a beloved brother.* Onesi-

mus is returning as someone different. A slave may be coming back, but he is to be regarded no longer *hōs doulon*, "as a slave." In this verse occurs the first mention of *doulos*, "slave," and it occurs here twice. To say that Onesimus was not really a slave in Paul's thinking would be to deny the force of this term. It expresses Onesimus' real legal status in life, and Paul is seeking to get him recognized as much more than that.

Paul is using here *hōs* to express a virtual equivalence, as he does elsewhere (e.g. v 17 *proslabou auton hōs eme*; 1 Thess 2:6 *hōs Christou apostoloi*, "as apostles of Christ"). It cannot mean "as if he were a slave," *pace* A. D. Callahan ("Paul's Epistle to Philemon," 373), because that would give the conjunction a contrary-to-fact nuance, which it does not have. Compare his *Embassy*, 44, where he mistranslates the text of Codex Claromontanus, *iam non quasi servum*, as "no longer a 'quasi slave.' " It simply means "no longer as a slave."

When Paul says "as a beloved brother," his argument in this letter reaches it first climax. So he pleads with Philemon on behalf of Onesimus. Paul employs the expression *adelphon agapēton*, "beloved brother," which is also found in 1 Cor 15:58; cf. Phil 4:1. On the connotation of *adelphos*, see NOTE on v 1. Recall too that in v 1 Paul greeted Philemon himself as *agapētos;* now he wants Philemon to regard Onesimus as such.

As a Christian, the slave is set in this way on a par with his master in the sight of the Lord (see Gal 3:28). He partakes with him of the Lord's Supper and shares with him the kiss of peace. So he is a "brother," because he is, like Philemon himself, a Christian, an adopted child of God through baptism (Gal 4:5; Rom 8:15), and a "new creature" (2 Cor 5:17). This is the fundamental appeal that Paul is making to Philemon, that he welcome Onesimus as a "brother," a fellow Christian. There is an intensification of Paul's argument here, in that he is implying strongly that Philemon should forgo punishing Onesimus.

Recall how in the OT a slave who is a Hebrew is called "brother" (Lev 25:39; Deut 15:12). For varied figurative uses of *adelphos*, see MM, 8–9. In the Stoic world, too, stress was put on the brotherhood of all human beings (see Seneca, *Ep.* 47.10; Epictetus, *Dissertationes* 1.13.3–4; 3.24.16).

A double contrast is expressed: a "slave" becomes a "beloved brother," and time is involved, "no longer . . . but (now)." The negative used is not the expected *mēketi* (in a purpose clause introduced by *hina*), but *ouketi* (negating the phrase *hōs doulon*), "no longer as a slave." It thus adds emphasis to the point of view that Paul wants Philemon to adopt.

Consequently, a triple possibility lies open before Philemon. He can take Onesimus back and punish him, as the law would allow. That is hardly what Paul is foreseeing. Or Philemon can take Onesimus back as a slave, restore him to the *familia*, and allow him to work and do his job in faithfulness and loyalty, as Col 3:22–4:1 prescribes (so Gnilka, Lohse, Lightfoot, and Nordling understand it). Or Philemon can emancipate Onesimus and send him as a Christian freedman back to help Paul in his evangelization (so Bartchy, Bruce, Koester, and Lohmeyer understand it). The last-mentioned possibility seems to be implied with subtlety by Paul, but he is in no way commanding it, as Collange and Stuhlmacher rightly insist. Whether the second or the third way of understanding what faces Philemon is better, the all-important element is that Onesimus be treated as "a beloved brother."

He is such to me. Lit. "exceedingly (beloved) to me." The adverb *malista,* "most of all," has to be understood in an elative sense because the following phrase "precludes its being literally superlative" (C. F. D. Moule, *Colossians and Philemon,* 148). Paul admits this because of what Onesimus has meant to him since his conversion. Lightfoot explains:

> The great capacity for good which appears in the typical slave of Greek and Roman fiction, notwithstanding all the fraud and profligacy overlying it, was evoked and developed here by the inspiration of a new faith and the incentive of a new hope. The genial, affectionate, winning disposition, purified and elevated by a higher knowledge, had found its proper scope. Altogether this new friendship was a solace and a strength to the Apostle in his weary captivity, which he could ill afford to forego. To take away Onesimus was to tear out Paul's heart. (*Colossians and Philemon,* 311)

but how much more to you. Paul recognizes the priority of the relationship of Onesimus to Philemon and acknowledges that Onesimus should be indeed beloved by Philemon to a degree that surpasses his own.

both as a human being and in the Lord. Lit. "both in the flesh and in the Lord." Paul alludes to Onesimus' ordinary condition as a man or a human being of this world (connoting his social and moral status), and also to his condition as a Christian, because he now exists *en Kyriō,* in union with the risen Lord. In both of these aspects Paul finds the good in Onesimus that he himself appreciates and that he hopes will be appreciated even more by Philemon. *Sarx* "denotes the circle of purely human relations irrespective of the fact that the slave and his master are also believers in the Lord's kingdom. The reference is to social relations rather than kinship. Here it is especially plain that the two spheres are not mutually exclusive. But the sphere of *sarx* is not the decisive one. It embraces the whole of human existence, both its bodily and its intellectual functions, though apart from the gracious gift of faith in the *kyrios*" (E. Schweizer, *TDNT,* 7. 127–28). See further Petersen, *Rediscovering Paul,* 174 n. 14.

Pace Callahan, *en sarki* here does not mean that Onesimus was a brother of Philemon "in the consanguinary sense" or as a "blood relative." It is merely Paul's way of stressing Onesimus' condition as a human being in contrast to his condition as a Christian. *Sarx* denotes, as often in Paul, that aspect of human life that is bound by earth-oriented interests, limited in its capacities, and affected by its appetites, ambitions, and proneness to sin (see A. Sand, *EDNT*, 3. 230–33, esp. 231). As used of Onesimus, the phrase *en sarki* expresses his basic human status apart from his condition as a slave; it is a status that Onesimus shares with Paul and Philemon, and Paul acknowledges that aspect of Onesimus' existence. "In the Lord," however, Onesimus' former condition and legal status may remain, but they are transformed by a life of spiritual dedication and obligation. For he has accepted the call to faith proclaimed in the gospel and has become a follower of Christ, a "freedman of the Lord."

Compare the contrasting phrase in Ignatius, *Trall.* 12.1: "who have refreshed me both in the flesh and in the spirit" (*sarki te kai pneumati*). See *TLNT*, 3. 236.

17. *If, then, you consider me your partner.* Or, "your comrade," i.e. one who shares your life and has common interests. The conjunction *ei* with the indicative expresses a simple condition (BDF §371.1; §372.1). Paul makes use of the noun *koinōnos*, which differs from *synergos*, "fellow worker," of v 1 (see NOTE there). It normally denotes "one who takes part in something with someone" (BAGD). Indeed, it may even have the nuance of one who is a partner in a common business pursuit or commercial endeavor (see 1 Thess 2:9 for an expression of Paul's toil and labor; 1 Cor 4:12 for his manual labor; cf. Luke 5:10). What Paul says in the following v 18 makes it likely that *koinōnos* means "partner," and then the common interests would involve not merely "faith and love," as Lohse has understood it (*Colossians and Philemon*, 203–4) but something more concrete, adding "a commercial dimension to the whole affair," as Dunn suggests (*Colossians and Philemon*, 336); similarly Campbell, *Three New Testament Studies*, 10.

welcome him as you would welcome me. Paul draws a conclusion from his argument thus far, as he entreats Philemon to receive Onesimus back kindly, because he has already identified the slave as his "very own heart" (v 12). Onesimus is to be welcomed as the virtual presence of Paul himself. This significant repetition of Paul's identification of himself with the slave Onesimus is based on his view of the unity of Christians in Christ (Gal 3:27–28) and *oikeioi tēs pisteōs*, "members of the household of faith" (Gal 6:10).

One now encounters the first imperative in the letter, *proslabou*, "welcome," the first expression of a command to Philemon. It is the first of four imperatives (see vv 18, 20, 22). The first two are found in the apodosis of conditional sentences.

For a similar recommendation of welcome, cf. Rom 15:7: "Welcome one another, then, as Christ welcomed you." Compare *P. Oxy.* 1. 32.6: *ut eum ant<e> oculos habeas tamquam me* (look upon him as if he were myself). Compare S. K. Stowers, *Letter Writing in Greco-Roman Antiquity* (Philadelphia, Pa.: Westminster, 1986) 157; *TLNT*, 3. 200. There is an echo of this verse in Ignatius, *Eph.* 6.1.

18. *If he has wronged you in any matter or owes you anything, charge that to me.* This is another simple condition parallel to that of v 17, in the apodosis of which the second imperative occurs. Paul states the matter hypothetically, but he realizes it to be true absolutely: Onesimus, he knows, has wronged Philemon in some way, possibly by dipping his hand into funds that were entrusted to him or by absconding with them; or in some other less serious way, in which Onesimus might have felt that he was being blamed for something for which he was not entirely at fault. Paul makes no mention of Onesimus' running away, or even of his remorse and regret. This too may be a reason why Paul states the case hypothetically.

Winter, however, believes that Paul is offering "to clear any possible debts that Onesimus would have outstanding with the Colossae household . . . in anticipation that" he "will be cutting all formal and legal ties to the household." That is hardly what this verse implies, because *se*, "you," is singular and the verb *ēdikēsen*, even if it stands in a conditional clause, refers to some harm that Onesimus might have done to Philemon himself.

The verb *adikein* means "do wrong to someone, treat someone unjustly," but sometimes it is used in the sense of financial wrongdoing (2 Pet 2:13), and here can mean theft, neglect of duty, or poor work (*TDNT*, 1. 161). Knox thinks that there is an allusion to *ēdikēsen* in Col 3:25, where it says that "the wrongdoer will be paid back for the wrong he has done" (*Philemon among the Letters*, 39), but that is clearly far-fetched.

The other two verbs, *opheilei*, "owes," and *elloga*, "charge," are examples of technical, commercial language that Paul introduces. The former is commonly used to express financial debts (see MM, 468–69), the latter to set something down to someone's account (MM, 204). The introduction of such language serves to express the close partnership between Paul and Philemon.

If Onesimus had been indeed a fugitive, he would be liable on his return to Philemon to serious punishment. That possibility, however, does not seem to be envisaged in either this or the following verse, where Paul promises to compensate Philemon on Onesimus' behalf. He is above all concerned that the two, Philemon and Onesimus, be reconciled; and so he is writing rather as *amicus domini* on behalf of a slave delinquent for a less serious cause.

How Paul would be able to recompense Philemon from his status as a prisoner is not explained, but he wants to be taken at his word. That is why he adds what appears in the next verse. This, in effect, makes Paul's letter a promissory note or security for payment. Possibly, Onesimus is ready to help Paul make this payment. Some commentators have understood this verse as if Paul were writing in a light vein, not intending what he says to be taken seriously: "Philemon will realize that the Apostle has no earthly riches at his disposal and will consequently understand what he means when he declares that he is prepared to stand good for the damages" (Lohse, *Colossians and Philemon,* 204; cf. Dibelius, *An Philemon,* 107: "mehr Scherz als Ernst"). That is an easy way of disposing of a problematic verse, as Stuhlmacher comments: "This is not meant only in a rhetorical way, as the following verse shows" (*Brief an Philemon,* 49; cf. Dunn, *Colossians and Philemon,* 339 n. 35).

The imperative *elloga,* "reckon (it) in, charge," is a strange form. It is usually understood to be a form of *ellogeō,* which has the same meaning, and an example of the confusion of contract verbs in *-an* and *-ein* in Koine Greek; cf. *ellogatai* in some MSS of Rom 5:13 (BDF §90; §123.2). Zerwick, however, considers it a form of *ellogaō,* with the same meaning (*GAGNT,* 2. 653), as does LSJ, 573. See further C. J. Martin, "The Rhetorical Function."

19. *I, Paul, write this with my own hand.* That is, it is an IOU, a holograph intended to assure Philemon about what he is saying and to guarantee him that the letter is not a falsification. This is also an indication that the letter is not merely a private communication to Philemon, but was envisaged by Paul as something that would be read to the church that gathered at Philemon's house.

Paul again introduces his own name, preceded by *egō,* to stress his personal involvement (cf. v 9; 2 Cor 10:1; Gal 5:2; 1 Thess 2:18; used in another sense in Col 4:18; 2 Thess 3:17). The verb *egrapsa* is again an epistolary aorist; see NOTE on v 7 and cf. Rom 15:15.

The whole of this short letter may be an autograph, as Jerome (PL 26. 651), Lightfoot (*Colossians and Philemon,* 342), Benoit ("Philémon," 1206), and Stuhlmacher (*Brief an Philemon,* 50 n. 122) have maintained; but if, in fact, Paul has been dictating the letter to a scribe, then at this point he may have snatched the pen and written at least this verse himself. Compare Col 4:18; Gal 6:17; 1 Cor 16:21. Bahr would begin Paul's writing in his own hand with v 17, but it is not clear why it would begin there (see "The Subscriptions," 35; cf. Roller, *Formular,* 592). *Pace* Knox (*Philemon among the Letters,* 35), this verse has no relation to the use of *cheirographon* in Col 2:14.

I will repay it. Paul repeats what he has already written in v 18, seeking to make Philemon feel sure that he, not Onesimus, will make up the loss. He uses *apotisō,* a technical juridical term for the payment of a fine or the cost of damages (see MM, 71).

not to mention. Lit. "that I may not say to you," with which an implied verb must be understood so that the *hina* clause is clearly final, even though it introduces what comes in the next clause (*IBNTG,* 145). The rhetorical figure of *praeteritio* or *paraleipsis* is used: Paul says he is passing over what he actually begins to say. Similarly in 2 Cor 9:4. Thus Paul transforms "Philemon's position from creditor to debtor and so . . . put[s] him under a limitless moral obligation to comply with Paul's requests" (J. M. G. Barclay, *NTS* 37 [1991]

172). See BDF §495.1 for a different, but less convincing, way of construing this Pauline remark.

that you owe me even your own self. Philemon apparently became a Christian through the evangelization of Paul so that he has become Philemon's spiritual father and patron, as well as that of Onesimus; he is saying, in fact, that Philemon is quite indebted to him. "With this phrase the language of debt and compensation no longer remains within the domain of juridical obligations, but is used in a figurative sense to describe the relationship of Philemon to the Apostle" (Lohse, *Colossians and Philemon,* 205). See further S. Bartina, " 'Me debes más' (Flm 19)," who stresses the difference between *ophelein* in v 18 and *prosophelein* here, which should mean "owe in addition"; cf. Lightfoot's translation, "owest besides" (*Colossians and Philemon,* 342). Paul's thought passes from the material debt that Onesimus may owe Philemon to the spiritual debt that Philemon does owe Paul. Even though Paul says this to Philemon in this letter that is also addressed to the church of Colossae that meets in his house, this is not to be taken as pressuring Philemon unduly. *Pace* Suhl (*Philemonbrief,* 39), Paul is not saying, "Do what I say; remember how much you owe me." Paul's language in this letter is much more subtle than that.

A certain amount of Greek vocabulary in vv 17–19 is common to Rom 15:25–27 (see Stuhlmacher, *Brief an Philemon,* 50 n. 126).

20. *Yes, my brother.* Paul addresses Philemon as *adelphe,* stressing again his fundamental Christian relationship to him; recall v 7. For a similar use of the adverb *nai,* "yes," see Phil 4:3; cf. BDF §432.1.

may I profit from you. Paul uses the optative *onaimēn* to express an attainable wish (BDF §384; *IBNTG,* 22, 136), which is almost an imperative in this context. He is pleading for Onesimus, but pleading also for his own work of evangelization. Lightfoot and Bahr think that the verb *onaimēn* involves another play on the name *Onēsimos,* but that is far from certain (see BDF §488.1b; Lohse, *Colossians and Philemon,* 205). Paul seeks only to get from Philemon some assistance in his evangelization in return for his sending Onesimus back to him, viz. the return of Onesimus to Paul as a helper (as he so appears in Col 4:9). Paul probably thought that this would not be a hardship for Philemon, who undoubtedly had other slaves in his household. Compare the similar use of *onaimēn* in Ignatius, *Eph.* 2.2.

in the Lord. Whatever profit Paul may get from Philemon is to be understood *en Kyriō,* "in the Lord," i.e. not in any secular sense. Note how these two short sentences both end in a prepositional phrase involving "the Lord" or "Christ."

Refresh my heart in Christ! Paul bids Philemon to show his true self. In effect, he repeats what he has said in the preceding sentence, but now recasts as an imperative the formula employed in the thanksgiving prayer of v 7. To it he adds *en Christō*, "in Christ," which stands in parallelism to "in the Lord" in the preceding sentence. Christ the Lord is thus the motivating force in Paul's appeal. On *splanchna*, translated as "heart," see NOTE on v. 7.

BIBLIOGRAPHY

Bahr, G. J., "The Subscriptions in the Pauline Letters," *JBL* 87 (1968) 27–41.

Bartina, S., " 'Me debes más' (Flm 19): La deuda de Filemón a Pablo," *SPCIC*, 2. 143–52.

Best, E., "Paul's Apostolic Authority—?" *JSNT* 27 (1986) 3–25, esp. 11–13.

Birdsall, J. N., "*Presbytēs* in Philemon 9: A Study in Conjectural Emendation," *NTS* 39 (1993) 625–30.

Crehan, J. H., "A New Fragment of Ignatius' *Ad Polycarpum*," *Studia patristica* (TU 63–64; ed. K. Aland and F. L. Cross; Berlin: Akademie-V., 1957), 1. 23–32.

Hauck, F., "*Opheilō, k.t.l.*," *TDNT*, 5. 559–66.

Malherbe, A. J., "Paulus Senex," *ResQ* 36 (1994) 197–207.

Marrow, S. B., *Speaking the Word Fearlessly: Boldness in the New Testament* (New York and Ramsey, N.J.: Paulist, 1982).

Martin, C. J., "The Rhetorical Function of Commercial Language in Paul's Letter to Philemon (Verse 18)," *Persuasive Artistry: Studies in New Testament Rhetoric in Honor of George A. Kennedy* (JSNTSup 50; ed. D. F. Watson; Sheffield, U.K.: JSOT, 1991) 321–37.

Mullins, T. Y., "Petition as a Literary Form," *NovT* 5 (1962) 46–54.

Pentecost, J. D., "For Love's Sake, Part III: An Exposition of Philemon 8–11," *BSac* 129 (1972) 344–51.

———, "Studies in Philemon, Part IV: Charge That to My Account," *BSac* 130 (1973) 50–57.

———, "Studies in Philemon, Part V: The Obedience of a Son," *BSac* 130 (1973) 164–70.

———, "Studies in Philemon, Part VI: Able to Keep You," *BSac* 130 (1973) 250–57.

Roller, O., *Das Formular der paulinischen Briefe* (BWANT 4/6; Stuttgart: Kohlhammer, 1933).

Schmidt, P., "Saulus der *neanias*," *Protestantische Monatshefte* 18 (1914) 156–58.

Steck, R., "Ein alter Paulus?" *Protestantische Monatshefte* 18 (1914) 96–100.

———, "Kein alter Paulus!" *Protestantische Monatshefte* 18 (1914) 192–93.

Stöger, A., "Fraternité: Phm 9b–10.12–17," *AsSeign* n.s. 54 (1972) 58–63.

IV. Conclusion (21–25)

[21]Confident of your acquiescence, I write to you, knowing that you will do even more than I ask. [22]At the same time, prepare a guest-room for me, for I hope that through your prayers I may be restored to you. [23]Epaphras, my fellow prisoner in Christ Jesus, sends you his greetings, [24]as do Mark, Aristarchus, Demas, and Luke, my fellow workers. [25]The grace of the Lord Jesus Christ be with your spirit!

COMMENT

Paul ends his letter with a final instruction, farewell greetings, and a blessing. He realizes that his plea in v 16 creates a problem, because it seeks to cut through a considerable amount of legality as he tries to bring Philemon to realize the status of the Christian slave that he is now sending back to him. Nevertheless he states his confidence in Philemon's acquiescence and pleads that he do "even more" than he asks. Furthermore, Paul announces that he hopes to be released soon from prison and to pay him a visit. In thus speaking of a coming visit, Paul again is applying subtle pressure; he may soon be on hand to see how Philemon has reacted to this letter and to his appeal for Onesimus. He speaks only of Philemon's acquiescence.

Did Philemon acquiesce? Col 4:9 would suggest that he did, because there Onesimus seems to be traveling freely with Tychicus and serving Paul.

In vv 23–24 Paul adds a list of the five collaborators who send along greetings with his own, and then in v 25 he utters a blessing over Philemon and his household. Note the similarity of the concluding greetings here with those in Col 4:10–14.

NOTES

21. *Confident of your acquiescence.* Lit. "being persuaded," a perfect participle that stresses Paul's abiding conviction (see *TLNT*, 3. 70, 76). His confidence is based on the faith that is common to Philemon and himself and on his relation to Philemon, already expressed at the end of v 19. He uses *hypakoē,* which generally means "obedience" and which Paul uses elsewhere of the commitment of Christian faith (Rom 1:5; 15:18; 16:26) or as a response to his apostolic authority (2 Cor 7:15; 10:5–6), but here it seems to be less strong,

while subtly expressing Philemon's willing compliance, for which Paul hopes. Paul presumes that Philemon will do as he asks. So Dibelius (*An Philemon*, 106) has understood the phrase; cf. *TLNT*, 1. 450 n. 64. Stuhlmacher, however, prefers the meaning "obedience," to which he thinks the letter has been building up (*Brief an Philemon*, 52–53), but that seems to be too strong an interpretation in light of what Paul has said about not wanting to exercise his authority (vv 8–9).

Gnilka notes that *hypakoē* has no object here and hence more plausibly suggests that the noun should be taken in the general Pauline sense of obedience to "the law of Christ" (Gal 6:2), and not obedience to Paul himself (*Philemonbrief*, 87–88). Nevertheless, this is not the only expression of confidence that Paul has written; see 2 Cor 1:15; 2:3; Gal 5:10; Phil 2:24. Compare S. N. Olson, "Pauline Expressions of Confidence"; see further Dunn, *Colossians and Philemon*, 344–45.

I write to you. Again *egrapsa* is an epistolary aorist; see NOTE on v 7. Dibelius (*An Philemon*, 107) queries whether the final greeting has been written by Paul's hand. Gnilka (*Philemonbrief*, 87) even interprets this statement as meaning most likely that Paul has written the whole letter himself.

knowing that you will do even more than I ask. Lit. "beyond what I say." Paul's argument reaches its second climax in the letter; see v 16 above for the first. His confidence now yields to knowledge. In v 16 the "more" has already been expressed: to accept Onesimus "as more than a slave, as a beloved brother." If vv 15–16 are not a plea that Philemon emancipate Onesimus or even hint at it, then here the "more" might imply manumission (see Lightfoot, *Colossians and Philemon*, 345). Paul would be hinting that Philemon should emancipate Onesimus and allow him to return to work with him as *libertus*. In Col 4:9, which was written some fifteen years later than this letter, Onesimus is already depicted as Paul's coworker. However, one cannot be certain, because even here Paul may be allowing Philemon to decide. According to Dibelius (*An Philemon*, 107), Paul is not even thinking about Onesimus' legal status. In other words, the ambiguity of the earlier verses (13–14, 16) is not resolved by the ambiguity of v 21.

The MSS א, A, C, P, 0278, 33, 81, 104 read *ha legō*, lit. "the things that I mention," whereas MSS D, Ψ, 1739 have the singular relative pronoun, *ho legō*, "what I mention." Paul uses the preposition *hyper*, "above, beyond," in a comparative sense meaning "more" (see BDF §230.1).

22. *At the same time, prepare a guest-room for me.* Lit. "prepare for me hospitality," an abstraction used for a concrete term. *Xenia* is used also in Acts 28:23 for Paul's "lodging" in Roman house-arrest, and is commonly found in Greek papyri (*P. Oxy.* 7. 1064.10; *TLNT*, 2. 560). Compare Pseudo-Clementine, *Hom.* 12.2.5–6; and Cicero, *Ad Atticum* 14.2: *Piliae paratum est hospitium* (hospitality has been prepared for Pilia). This request of Paul is scarcely a

"throwaway remark," as Dunn would have it (*Colossians and Philemon*, 347), for it adds emphasis to his plea for Onesimus, implying that Paul will find Onesimus well restored to his place in the household when he at length comes to the Lycus Valley to visit Philemon, whenever that may be. Then Paul would be able to see how Philemon has reacted to his letter and to his plea for Onesimus. This request is also a way of expressing his coming *parousia*, even though in this case his presence may be less characterized by apostolic authority (see R. W. Funk, "The Apostolic *Parousia*").

The adverb *hama* is used with an imperative (BDF §425.2; *IBNTG*, 82). For the strangeness of a present imperative in this context, see *IBNTG*, 135.

Did Paul succeed in visiting Philemon after release from prison? Or did he go directly on to Macedonia, as Acts 20:1–3 may suggest? Gnilka (*Philemonbrief*, 90) thinks that the latter is more likely. This verse especially creates a problem for those commentators who think that Paul writes from his Roman house-arrest. How would his plans as expressed here fit in with his intention to go from Rome to Spain (Rom 15:24, 28)?

for I hope that through your prayers I may be restored to you. Lit. "that through your (plural) prayers I may be graciously given to you (plural)," i.e. as an answer to those prayers. Thus Paul expresses his epistolary hope, as in Rom 15:24; 1 Cor 16:7; Phil 1:25; 2:19, 23. He means thereby his own speedy release from prison, and for that he asks Philemon and the church that gathers at his house to pray and petition heaven. Paul seeks God's help in his current situation, begging Philemon and the others to intercede for him. Compare G. P. Wiles, *Paul's Intercessory Prayers* (SNTSMS 24; Cambridge: Cambridge University, 1974) 282. Diodorus Siculus (13.59.3) uses the same verb *charizesthai* in the sense of setting captives free. Contrast the use of *charizesthai* in Acts 3:14; 25:16, where it has a different (negative) connotation of "handing someone over to somebody else."

23. *Epaphras.* With this verse Paul lists those who send greetings to Philemon and the other addressees, as was customary in ancient letters (see Roller, *Formular*, 472–74).

The first named is Epaphras, the evangelist of the Lycus Valley, a coworker of Paul. In Col 1:7 he is depicted as Paul's "beloved fellow slave" and "faithful minister of Christ" for the sake of the Colossians. In Col 4:12 he is described as "one of yourselves," i.e. a native of Colossae, and "a slave of Christ [Jesus]," one who has worked hard for the Christians of Laodicea and Hierapolis. In Col 1:7–8 he seems to be considered the founder of the Colossian church, and this is undoubtedly why he is mentioned first.

Epaphras is a shortened form of *Epaphroditus* (Phil 2:25; 4:18; cf. BDF §125.1), someone named after Aphrodite, a pagan goddess; so he was most likely a Gentile Christian. He later became a bishop of Colossae and a martyr for the Christian faith (feast day in the Roman Martyrology: July 19).

my fellow prisoner in Christ Jesus. In Col 4:10 the term *synaichmalōtos,* "fellow prisoner," is used of Aristarchus, who is mentioned by Luke in Acts 27:2 as traveling with the prisoner Paul to Rome. The term is given here to Epaphras, who may not have been a "fellow prisoner" of Paul in the same sense, as Stuhlmacher (*Brief an Philemon,* 55) prefers to understand it. The term may be employed only in a figurative sense here, meaning that both Paul and Epaphras are prisoners of Christ; cf. 2 Cor 2:14 ("Christ always leads us in triumph"). The same use of the term is found in Rom 16:7 of Andronicus and Junia. On the meaning of *synaichmalōtos,* see T. da Castel S. Pietro, "*Synaichmalōtos.*"

Lohse (*Colossians and Philemon,* 207 n. 16) considers it unique that Paul says here "my fellow prisoner in Christ Jesus," and prefers an old conjecture, which reads only *en Christō,* followed by the nominative *Iēsous* (instead of the genitive *Iēsou,* of all the Greek MSS). That would mean that Paul considered Epaphras as his "fellow prisoner in Christ" and that someone named "Jesus" would also be sending greetings, as in Col 4:11. So too argues Zahn (*Introduction to the New Testament,* 1. 459). That reading, however, is highly arbitrary, as Gnilka notes (*Philemonbrief,* 92 n. 8), because the person in Col 4:11 is actually *Iēsous ho legomenos Ioustos,* "Jesus, called Justus," and the conjecture dismisses the value of the Greek manuscripts (so too Stuhlmacher, *Brief an Philemon,* 55). E. Amling ("Eine Konjektur") even claims that a scribal error is responsible for the omission of Jesus Justus in this letter, a suggestion that Knox (*Philemon among the Letters,* 35) considers plausible.

sends you his greetings. For the use of *aspazesthai,* "greet," as an expression of a distinct literary form in ancient Greek letters, see T. Y. Mullins, "Greeting." The greetings of Epaphras are conveyed to Philemon in the singular, as Paul has been addressing him elsewhere since v 5, apart from v 22, where the second person shifted momentarily to the plural.

24. *as do Mark.* In Col 4:10 Mark is identified as the cousin of Barnabas. As there, Mark is mentioned in second place here. This is "John, who is called Mark," a Jewish Christian, the sometime collaborator of Paul mentioned in Acts 12:12, 25; 13:13; 15:37–39. He is still mentioned in later NT writings, such as Col 4:10; 2 Tim 4:11; 1 Pet 5:13. To him Christian tradition has ascribed the Second Gospel, the preaching of the gospel in Alexandria, and martyrdom there in the eighth year of Nero (see Jerome, *De viris inlustribus* 8 [PL 23.654]).

Aristarchus. Undoubtedly the same person as the one mentioned in Col 4:10–11 and described as Paul's "fellow prisoner" and a Jewish Christian. Whereas he is the first mentioned in that Colossian passage, he is the third in this letter. Aristarchus is mentioned also in the Lucan story of Paul in Acts 19:29; 20:4; 27:2 and identified there as "a Macedonian from Thessalonica," who accompanies Paul. In later Christian tradition he became a bishop of Thessalonica and a martyr.

Demas. In Col 4:14 *Dēmas*, a Gentile Christian, sends greetings to the Colossians. He is probably the same as the one named here, and in 2 Tim 4:10, where he is said to have deserted Paul. Epiphanius relates that he became a pagan priest (*Panarion* 51.6.7), and this has been repeated by Photius of Constantinople (K. Staab, *Pauluskommentare,* 637). In Ignatius, *Magn.* 2.1, a bishop of Magnesia named *Damas* is mentioned, and some commentators think that he is the same as the Demas who sends greetings here; but that is problematic, because the spelling is different and it contradicts Epiphanius' report. *Dēmas* is probably a shortened form of *Dēmētrios.*

Luke. In Col 4:14 *Loukas* is mentioned next to last and described as "the beloved physician," a Gentile Christian. Compare 2 Tim 4:11, where he is said to be alone with "Paul." Early Christian tradition ascribed to this Luke the Third Gospel (and Acts) and his origin in Antioch in Syria. See further Fitzmyer, *Luke,* AB, 35–41; cf. W. Ramsay, *St. Paul the Traveller and the Roman Citizen* (London: Hodder and Stoughton, 1895) 202–5, who thinks that Luke "was resident in Troas" and "had some connection with Philippi."

my fellow workers. So Paul describes the five companions who send greetings to Philemon and the other addressees. As was Philemon (see v 1), they have all been bound to Paul as helpers and now undoubtedly support Paul's appeal to Philemon about Onesimus. Recall Rom 16:3, 9, 21, where the same designation is used of other helpers of Paul. They are not necessarily to be understood as prisoners along with Paul, *pace* Suhl (*Paulus,* 168 n. 92).

25. *The grace of the Lord Jesus Christ be with your spirit!* See Gal 6:18; Phil 4:23, where Paul concludes his letters to others similarly; cf. 1 Thess 5:28; 1 Cor 16:23–24; 2 Cor 13:13; Rom 16:20b. He never uses the standard greeting of secular letters (*errōso* [singular] or *errōsthe* [plural], "Farewell!"), which is found in Acts 15:29; but he invariably formulates his farewell in terms of "grace." In effect, Paul prays that divine favor will be shown to all the addressees (of vv 1–2) so that they, along with Philemon, may learn the lesson of love and come to the same compliance (*hypakoē,* v 21) as he. Consequently, this blessing repeats the greeting of v 3, extending it now to all the addressees mentioned in vv 1–2. Paul reverts again to the plural *hymōn,* "your." In writing *meta tou pneumatos hymōn,* "with your spirit," he employs *pneuma* in an anthropological sense as synecdoche; it does not refer to the Holy Spirit. See Phil 4:23, and also *TDNT,* 6. 435, for instances where *pneuma* is used in a concluding salutation, whereas parallels employ rather *meth' hymōn,* "with you" (plural). In using "spirit," the thought is expressed in a more Hebraic form (see E. Schweizer, *TDNT,* 6. 435).

MSS A, C, D, Ψ, 0278, and the Koine text-tradition add *hēmōn,* "our (Lord)," but that possessive pronoun is omitted in MSS א, P, 33, 81, 104, 365, 1739, 1881, and it is not used in Phil 4:23. MSS א, C, D^1, Ψ, 0278, 1739, and the Koine text-tradition add at the end *Amēn.* That probably comes from a contemporary liturgical custom of adding a response to the end of the reading of an epistle; but MSS A, D*, 048, 33, 81, 1881 do not follow suit. In the use of such formulas, liturgical practice often induced modifications. It is not impossible that the omission is owing to haplography, since both words end in *-n (hymōn. Amēn.)*. See *TCGNT*, 589. Luther concludes his comments on the Letter to Philemon thus:

> Thus we have a private epistle from which much should be learned how brethren are to be commended, that is, that an example might be provided to the church how we ought to take care of those who fall and restore those who err; for the kingdom of Christ is a kingdom of mercy and grace, while the kingdom of Satan is a kingdom of murder, error, darkness, and lies. (tr. J. Pelikan, *LW*, 29. 105)

At the end of the letter, various so-called subscriptions (*subscriptiones*) supply details about the place whence the letter was sent or identify some of the persons who are named in it. The purpose of the subscription was to mark the end of the writing. In this case, the various subscriptions are found in different Greek MSS:

Pros Philemona alone (MSS ℵ, A, C, Ψ, 33), "To Philemon."
Pros Philēmona egraphē (MSS D, E), "(the letter) was written to Philemon."
Pros Philēmona apo Rōmēs (MSS P, 048), "To Philemon from Rome."
Pros Philēmona kai Apphian despotas tou Onēsimou kai pros Archippon ton diakonon tēs en Kolossais ekklēsias (MSS L, 101, Syr^{h}), "To Philemon and Apphia, masters of Onesimus, and to Archippus, the deacon of the church in Colossae."
egraphē apo Rōmēs dia (+ *Tychikou kai* [MSS L, 1739, 1881]) *Onēsimou oiketou* [MS 1739] (+ *phygados* [MS 1881]), "it was written from Rome (and carried) by (Tychicus and) Onesimus, the household servant" (+ "the fugitive").

One subscription names *Tertoullos*, "Tertullus," the Roman eparch under whom Onesimus is said to have suffered martyrdom (see BAGD, 813; also *TCGNT*, 589–90).

BIBLIOGRAPHY

Amling, E., "Eine Konjektur im Philemonbrief," ZNW 10 (1909) 261–62.
Castel S. Pietro, T. da, "*Synaichmalōtos*: Compagno di prigionia o conquistato assieme? (Rom. 16,7; Col. 4,10; Filem. 23)," *SPCIC*, 2. 417–28.
Funk, R. W., "The Apostolic *Parousia*: Form and Significance," *Christian His-*

tory and Interpretation: Studies Presented to John Knox (ed. W. R. Farmer et al.; Cambridge: Cambridge University, 1967) 249–68.

Haykin, M. A. G., "Praying Together: A Note on Philemon 22," *EvQ* 66 (1994) 331–35.

Mullins, T. Y., "Greeting as New Testament Form," *JBL* 87 (1968) 418–26.

———, "Visit Talk in New Testament Letters," *CBQ* 35 (1973) 350–58.

Olson, S. N., "Pauline Expressions of Confidence in His Addressees," *CBQ* 47 (1985) 282–95.

Weima, J. A. D., *Neglected Endings: The Significance of the Pauline Letter Closings* (JSNTSup 101; Sheffield, U.K.: Academic Press, 1994) 230–36.

INDEX OF SUBJECTS

◆

INDEX

Index of Commentators and Modern Authors

(N.B. ä is treated as ae, ö as oe, ü as ue, m' and mc as mac)

◆

INDEX

INDEX

Index of Biblical and Other Ancient Writings

◆

OLD TESTAMENT (with Apocrypha)

NEW TESTAMENT

NONCANONICAL EARLY CHRISTIAN LITERATURE

NONCANONICAL JEWISH WRITINGS

GREEK CLASSICAL LITERATURE

LATIN CLASSICAL LITERATURE